D1270063

THE DOCTORS OF THE CHURCH
Volume One

BY THE SAME AUTHOR

Moments in Catholic History

Traveling with Jesus in the Holy Land

Married Saints

The Mission and Future of the Catholic Press (Editor)

Visit our website at
WWW.ALBAHOUSE.ORG

The Doctors of the Church

*An Introduction to
the Church's Great Teachers*

VOLUME ONE:
DOCTORS OF THE FIRST MILLENNIUM

JOHN F. FINK

ALBA·HOUSE   NEW·YORK

SOCIETY OF ST. PAUL, 2187 VICTORY BLVD., STATEN ISLAND, NEW YORK 10314

ST PAULS

Library of Congress Cataloging-in-Publication Data

Fink, John F.
    The doctors of the Church : an introduction to the Church's
great teachers / John F. Fink.
        p. cm.
    Contents: v. 1. Doctors of the first millennium — v. 2. Doctors
of the second millennium.
    ISBN 0-8189-0841-6 (set) — ISBN 0-8189-0839-4 (v. 1) —
ISBN 0-8189-0840-8 (v.2)
        1. Doctors of the Church—Biography. 2. Doctors of the
church. I. Title.

    BX4669.F56 2000
    282—dc21   99-089279

Produced and designed in the United States of America by the
Fathers and Brothers of the Society of St. Paul,
2187 Victory Boulevard, Staten Island, New York 10314-6603,
as part of their communications apostolate.

ISBN: 0-8189-0839-4 Doctors of the Church, Volume 1.
ISBN: 0-8189-0840-8 Doctors of the Church, Volume 2.
ISBN: 0-8189-0841-6 Doctors of the Church, 2 Volume Set.

Printing Information:

Current Printing - first digit   1   2   3   4   5   6   7   8   9   10

Year of Current Printing - first year shown

2000   2001   2002   2003   2004   2005   2006   2007   2008

DEDICATION

To Marie and Our Children:

Regina
Barbara
Robert
Stephen
Therese
David
John

TABLE OF CONTENTS

INTRODUCTION

No, this isn't a book about the great healers in the history of the Catholic Church. Although we sometimes seem to think of doctors as physicians, or perhaps dentists, the word "doctor" actually comes from the Latin *docere*, which means to teach. Historically, as those in academic communities know, "doctor" has been the title of an accomplished teacher. Today a doctorate remains the highest academic degree in a particular field.

In the Catholic Church, the title "Doctor of the Church" has been given to a relatively small number of men and women — thirty-three, to be exact — whose combination of intellectual brilliance and sanctity has been of extraordinary importance in the development of doctrine or spirituality. All of them have made lasting contributions to the understanding of the Catholic faith and are recognized for their great merits. However, the title does not necessarily infer that everything they wrote is free of errors.

The Church has recognized three categories of outstanding Christian writers: the Apostolic Fathers, the Fathers of the Church, and the Doctors of the Church. The Apostolic Fathers were Christian writers of the first and second centuries whose writings were derived from Christ's Apostles. Chief among them are Saint Clement, the third successor of Saint Peter as bishop of Rome; Saint Ignatius of Antioch, the second successor of Saint Peter in that see and a disciple of Saint John the Apostle; and Saint Polycarp, bishop of Smyrna and another disciple of Saint John. The unknown authors of the *Didache*, an important record of Christian belief, practice and governance from the second century, are also considered to be Apostolic Fathers.

The Fathers of the Church were theologians and writers of the first eight centuries who were known for their learning and holiness. Some were popes while others were lawyers, theologians, monks or hermits. Depending upon what list you consult, there were about a hundred Fathers of the Church, usually divided between Greek Fathers and Latin Fathers. This division was not only by language but by whether they lived in the Eastern or Western worlds. They also were sometimes divided between Ante-Nicene Fathers, who lived before the Council of Nicaea in 325; the Nicene Fathers who guided the Church during the fourth century when so much doctrine was formulated; and Post-Nicene Fathers, who lived after the fourth century.

Obviously, not all one hundred or so of these Fathers of the Church were equal in their learning or influence on the Church. Therefore, the greatest of the Fathers were also considered to be the Doctors of the Church. Initially, the Doctors were considered to be Saints Augustine, Ambrose, Jerome, and Pope Gregory I (the Great). However, they were all from the West, so later four men from the East were added: Saints Athanasius, Basil, Gregory Nazianzen, and John Chrysostom. All of them lived between 297 (the date of Athanasius's birth) and 604 (when Gregory the Great died).

These eight men, then, were commonly recognized as the Doctors of the Church at least from the eighth century until the sixteenth century. Then, in 1567, Pope Pius V (now Saint Pius V) wanted to honor Saint Thomas Aquinas in a special way and he added him to the list of Doctors. Saint Bonaventure was added in 1588. The list remained at ten until the 1720's. Saint Anselm was added in 1720, Saint Isidore of Seville in 1722, and Saint Peter Chrysologus in 1729. Saint Leo the Great was added in 1754.

More than half of the Doctors were named during the nineteenth and twentieth centuries— nine in the nineteenth century and ten in the twentieth. Those honored in the 1800's were Saints Peter Damian, 1828; Bernard of Clairvaux, 1830; Francis de Sales, 1877; Cyril of Alexandria and Cyril of Jerusalem, both in 1882; John Damascene, 1890;

and Bede, 1899. Those named during the twentieth century were Saints Ephrem of Syria, 1920;
Peter Canisius, 1925; John of the Cross, 1926; Robert Bellarmine and Albert the Great, both in 1931;
Anthony of Padua, 1946; Lawrence of Brindisi,
1959; Teresa of Avila and Catherine of Siena, both
in 1970; and Thérèse of Lisieux, 1997.

The list was an all-male club until 1970 and
even today, although the last three named to the
list were women, men Doctors outnumber women
Doctors thirty to three.

Some of the Doctors have been honored with
special titles. Saint Augustine is known as *Doctor
Gratiae*, Doctor of Grace, because of the importance of his writings about the theology of grace.
Saint Thomas Aquinas is known as both *Doctor
Angelicus*, the Angelic Doctor, and *Doctor Com-
munis*, the Common Doctor, the latter to denote
his universality and timeliness to all who study the
Church's teachings. Saint Anselm earned the title
of *Doctor Marianus*, the Marian Doctor, through
his writings about the Blessed Virgin Mary and her
role in salvation history. Saint Bernard of Clairvaux
is known as *Doctor Mellifluus*, the Mellifluous
Doctor, because of his sweet but powerful preaching. Saint Bonaventure is referred to as *Doctor
Seraphicus*, the Seraphic Doctor, because he was
a Franciscan and Saint Francis once had a vision
in which the crucified Christ was borne aloft by
Seraphim. Finally, Saint Albert the Great is known

as *Doctor Universalis*, the Universal Doctor, because of the vast extent of his theological and philosophical work.

In the chapters that follow, I will give profiles of each of the thirty-three Doctors of the Church. Each profile will be followed by one or more writings from that particular Doctor. Needless to say, the profiles cannot be full biographies and the writings can be little more than samples since this book is intended to be only a popular introduction to the Doctors of the Church. As one would expect, the writings of most of the Doctors are voluminous. I tried to choose excerpts that are representative of that particular Doctor's writings, but I also tried to choose works that would give an overall effect of providing a fairly thorough overview of Christian doctrine and practice through the centuries.

I chose to write about them in roughly chronological, rather than alphabetical order, in order to place them in their historical context and because some of the Doctors worked with, or were influenced by, other Doctors of the same era.

I hope, of course, that readers will want to read more of the writings of these Doctors of the Church and will avail themselves of opportunities to do so.

FOREWORD
TO VOLUME ONE

Seventeen of the thirty-three men and women who
have been declared Doctors of the Church lived
in the first millennium. Thirteen of those seventeen lived and taught in the fourth or fifth century
— through St. Leo the Great. The other four did
the writing for which they were declared Doctors
in the seventh and eighth centuries. None of the
theologians and Church leaders of the ninth and
tenth centuries have been declared Doctors.

The earliest of the Doctors of the Church were
writing at the same time as the Church began holding ecumenical councils to decide what were true
doctrines and what were heresies. The dogmas that
the Catholic Church holds today were determined
and defined by those councils, and the writings of
the Doctors of the Church were largely responsible
for the reasoning behind the councils' decisions.

The early Christians had a tough time trying
to understand just who Jesus was. Until he appeared on earth, no one had any idea that God was
more than one person. The Jews believed in one
God, and one person, while the pagan gentiles

believed in many gods, each of them a separate person. Only Christians believe both that there is only one God but that he is more than one person — the Father, the Son and the Holy Spirit — and that Jesus, as one of those persons, was both divine and human.

It took the Catholic Church all of about seven hundred fifty years to come to terms with those fundamental mysteries and doctrines — during the lives of all seventeen of the Doctors of the Church profiled in this volume. It didn't take that long for the Church to decide the mysteries and doctrines, but it took that long to combat the heresies that kept coming up when certain individuals tried to understand how Jesus could be both God and man and, in the process, came to wrong conclusions.

It isn't surprising that the first Doctors of the Church appeared at the beginning of the fourth century. It was at that time that the Christians were able to come out of their catacombs. For 250 years their Church had endured persecutions from the Roman emperors. Now, with Constantine's Edict of Milan in 323, they were actually free to practice their religion openly. Constantine also convened the first ecumenical council, the First Council of Nicaea, in 325.

It's not that there weren't Christian teachers prior to the fourth century. There were some very important writers, starting with the evangelists who wrote the Gospels, St. Paul who wrote his epistles, and the other authors of the New Testament. Other important writers prior to the fourth century include Ignatius of Antioch, Polycarp, Justin, Irenaeus, Clement of Alexandria, Origen, Tertullian, Hippolytus, and Cyprian. All of these men are considered to be Fathers of the Church but were never declared Doctors.

There were also heresies prior to the fourth century, some of them, in fact, expounded by some of the Fathers of the Church — notably Hippolytus and Origen. Of course, none of the founders of the heresies believed that they were heresies. Hippolytus (170-236), for example, was so convinced that he was correct in his beliefs that he set himself up as the first antipope. He was convinced that the pope, Callistus, was too lenient because he admitted to Communion those who had already done penance for murder, adultery, and fornication, and those who had apostatized during persecution. Nevertheless, Hippolytus was perhaps the most important theologian and prolific writer before the age of Constantine. He was eventually reconciled to the Church and is honored as a saint.

Origen (185-254), who succeeded Clement as head of the Catechetical School of Alexandria, was author of a vast number of writings and some of the Doctors of the Church held him in high esteem. He was considered orthodox during his lifetime, but after his death, St. Jerome accused him of heresy and succeeded in having Pope Anastasius condemn some of his writings in 400.

Some of the most notable heresies prior to the fourth century were Docetism, Gnosticism, Marcionism, Montanism, Donatism, Sabellianism, and Manichaeism. But none of those heresies had the effect on Church history that Arianism did. This was the principal heresy of the fourth century and the one that all the earliest Doctors of the Church had to combat. The reason this heresy was so strong is that it was defended by some of the emperors of the Roman Empire, despite the condemnation of the heresy by popes and councils. Even after it was condemned by the First Council of Nicaea, there were more Arian bishops than orthodox.

This is a heresy, by the way, that continues to exist in Christianity yet today, although those who profess it don't call themselves Arians. Nevertheless, all those Christians who say that they believe that Jesus was a great man, but not God, could be called Arians because they deny the divinity of Christ.

Of the seventeen Doctors of the Church during the first millennium, eight came from the Eastern Church while nine were from the West. (All sixteen of the Doctors during the second millennium were from the West, in fact, from Europe.) Somehow it seems appropriate that both the first and the last Doctors of the first millennium (Saints Athanasius and John Damascene, respectively) were from the East, where Christianity began.

BIBLIOGRAPHY AND ACKNOWLEDGMENTS

It would be impossible to list all the many lives of saints that include biographies of some, or all, of the Doctors of the Church. I will, therefore, simply list those that I consulted during the writing of this volume:

I always read over the biography of the Doctor I was going to write about in *Butler's Lives of the Saints*, which was originally published in 1756-9, revised in 1926-38, and subsequent editions published in 1956, 1966, 1981 and 1982. HarperCollins published the edition I used in 1991.

Also helpful was a two-volume *Lives of Saints* published in 1953 and 1963 by John J. Crawley & Co. The company is no longer in existence and the books are out of print. Not all of the Doctors of the Church are in them, but some are. I also consulted *Saint of the Day*, a popular book published by St. Anthony Messenger Press. In addition, *The Oxford Dictionary of Popes*, published by Oxford University Press, was helpful for the lives of Popes Leo the Great and Gregory the Great, and the book *Saint Augustine*, by Garry Wills, published by Lipper/Viking, served the same purpose for the chapter about Saint Augustine.

I also checked facts in three books published by Our Sunday Visitor Press: *Catholic Almanac*, *Encyclopedia of Saints,* and *Encyclopedia of Catholic History.* And to check historical facts, I used *The Oxford Illustrated History of Christianity*, published by Oxford University Press. I also found *An Outline History of the Church by Centuries*, published by B. Herder Book Co. way back in 1943, still valuable today.

The excerpts from the Doctors of the Church are, of course, from their writings. I should note that I kept the Scripture quotations in those excerpts as they were already quoted rather than use any of the modern translations.

For readers who would like to read more by the Doctors, I suggest they check their libraries and Catholic bookstores. Some of the writings, especially some of those by Saint Augustine, are more available than others. One extremely valuable place to read more from the Doctors, as well as writings from other saints, is the Office of Readings, part of the Liturgy of the Hours that all Catholics are encouraged to pray.

THE DOCTORS OF THE CHURCH
Volume One

SAINT ATHANASIUS

Of all the Doctors of the Church, Saint Athanasius probably lived the most tumultuous life. None of the others were exiled from their position five times and none of the others had to spend six years hiding among monks in the Egyptian desert because people wanted to kill him. People took religious controversy very seriously in those days.

Athanasius probably was born in 297 in Alexandria, Egypt. He received a good education which included Greek literature and philosophy, and Christian doctrine. About the year 318 he was ordained to the diaconate and made secretary to Bishop Alexander of Alexandria. It was most likely during this time that he composed his first literary work, a treatise on the Incarnation, an excerpt from which is included below.

As I noted in the Foreword, the early Christians had a difficult time trying to understand who Jesus was and many sincere people had different opinions. Earnest and very religious people ended up being condemned as heretics when they proposed ways to understand the Incarnation. By far the most difficult heresy for early Christianity was Arianism. It is named after Arius, another priest from Alexandria. He denied the divinity of Christ by proclaiming that the Word was not eternal with the Father but was a creature of the Father. Arianism quickly spread and was threatening to destroy the Church.

In 324 Constantine became sole ruler of the Roman Empire. He promptly declared religious freedom, releasing Christianity from persecution by the Romans. Besides bringing Christianity out of the catacombs and building churches in Rome and in the Holy Land, he considered himself divinely commissioned to secure the Church's unity. Although he wasn't the pope (Sylvester I was), or a bishop, or even a baptized Christian yet, he called what is regarded as the first ecumenical council, the Council of Nicaea, in 325. It was held in a lakeside town near Constantine's palace in Constantinople (present-day Istanbul, Turkey).

Between 200 and 300 bishops from many countries attended the council (one was Bishop Nicholas of Myra, who was destined to go down in history as Santa Claus). Constantine invited Pope Sylvester to attend along with all other bishops, but he declined and sent two priests to represent him.

Athanasius was at the council as Bishop Alexander's archdeacon and secretary. After much argumentation the council condemned Arianism and accepted an official creed, adopting the language proposed by Athanasius. Modified by later councils, this became the Nicene Creed that Catholics recite at Mass on Sundays. The council anathematized anyone who said there was a time when the Son of God did not exist or that he was in any way different in substance from the Father.

The bishops at the council thought they had won the battle when they condemned Arianism. They soon learned, though, that they hadn't succeeded in quashing this heresy. As was to happen over and over after councils, many Christians ignored the decisions of the council. Rather than die, Arianism spread rapidly. Even Constantine, who called the Council of Nicaea, was baptized while on his deathbed by an Arian bishop — Eusebius of Nicomedia, who proved to be Athanasius's strongest opponent. Arians and semi-Arians established their own hierarchies and churches, and caused a great deal of trouble for several centuries. Saint Jerome later noted, "The world groaned and marveled to find that it was Arian."

Bishop Alexander died shortly after the Council of Nicaea and Athanasius was chosen to succeed him as Bishop of Alexandria. From then on he was the most outspoken champion for the doctrine that Jesus was God. The Arian bishops, though, had the ear of Emperor Constantine, who ordered Athanasius to re-admit Arius into communion. Athanasius refused and this so infuriated the

Arians that they accused him of some trumped-up crimes. In a trial before the emperor himself, Athanasius cleared himself — this time.

In 335, though, Athanasius was summoned to appear before another court at Tyre. He complied but, when he realized that his fate had been determined beforehand, he left the assembly and went to Constantinople. There he managed to get an interview with Constantine, who wrote a letter to the Council of Tyre summoning them to Constantinople for a retrial. However, a second letter from the council arrived announcing that Athanasius was to be exiled to Trier in Belgian Gaul — the first of his five exiles.

Constantine died in 337 and his empire was divided among his three sons: Constantine II, Constantius and Constans. One of Constantine II's first acts was to recall Athanasius to his see. But Bishop Eusebius won over Emperor Constantius, within whose jurisdiction Alexandria was situated. Eusebius also managed to obtain from a council at Antioch a second sentence of deposition against Athanasius. The council also ratified an Arian bishop for Alexandria, a man named Gregory.

Athanasius then went to Rome to have his case heard by the pope. Julius I called a synod which completely vindicated Athanasius, a verdict later endorsed by the Council of Sardica. He returned to Alexandria in triumph in 346 and there was comparative peace for four years. But when

Constans was murdered in 350 Constantius found himself ruler of both West and East and set himself to crush the man he now regarded as his enemy — Athanasius. Constantius managed to obtain the condemnation of Athanasius from a council at Arles in 353 and another at Milan in 355. This time Pope Liberius was brought to Milan by force and brainwashed into acquiescing in Athanasius's excommunication. (Once freed, though, he recanted.) In Alexandria, soldiers forced their way into the church and killed some of the congregation. Athanasius escaped and spent the next six years moving about among the monks in the desert, who protected him.

After Constantius died in 361 the new emperor, Julian the Apostate, at first revoked the sentence of banishment. But soon he realized that his efforts to re-paganize the empire required him to get rid of Athanasius, who experienced his fourth exile. Julian was succeeded by Emperor Jovian, who recalled Athanasius. But Jovian didn't last long as emperor and the next emperor, Valens, again ordered all orthodox bishops exiled. This exile was for only four months, though, and in September 365 Athanasius was welcomed back with great demonstrations of joy. He had spent a total of seventeen years in exile but was able to spend the last seven years of his life in peace. He died on May 2, 373.

Athanasius is known as the "Father of Orthodoxy" because of his efforts at defeating Arianism. His writings lay the groundwork for the second ecumenical council, the Council of Constantinople of 381, at which Arianism was again condemned.

His biography of Saint Anthony of Egypt was also a best-seller of his day, encouraging many Christians to become hermits in the desert.

Cardinal John Henry Newman said that Athanasius stands as "a principal instrument after the Apostles by which the sacred truths of Christianity have been conveyed and secured to the world."

The Church celebrates his feast on May 2.

From *On the Incarnation*, by Saint Athanasius

The Word of God, incorporeal, incorruptible and immaterial, entered our world. Yet it was not as if he had been remote from it up to that time. For there is no part of the world that was ever without his presence; together with his Father, he continually filled all things and places.

Out of his loving kindness for us he came to us, and we see this in the way he revealed himself openly to us. Taking pity on mankind's weakness, and moved by our corruption, he could not stand aside and see death have the mastery over us; he did not want creation to perish and his

Father's work in fashioning man to be in vain. He therefore took to himself a body, no different from our own, for he did not wish simply to be in a body or only to be seen.

If he had wanted simply to be seen, he could indeed have taken another, and nobler, body. Instead, he took our body in its reality.

Within the Virgin he built himself a temple, that is, a body; he made it his own instrument in which to dwell and to reveal himself. In this way he received from mankind a body like our own, and, since all were subject to the corruption of death, he delivered this body over to death for all, and with supreme love offered it to the Father. He did so to destroy the law of corruption passed against all men, since all died in him. The law, which had spent its force on the body of the Lord, could no longer have any power against his fellowmen. Moreover, this was the way in which the Word was to restore mankind to immortality, after it had fallen into corruption, and summon it back from death to life. He utterly destroyed the power death had against mankind — as fire consumes chaff — by means of the body he had taken and the grace of the Resurrection.

This is the reason why the Word assumed a body that could die, so that this body, sharing in the Word who is above all, might satisfy death's requirement in place of all. Because of the Word dwelling in that body, it would remain incorruptible, and all would be freed forever from corruption by the grace of the Resurrection.

In death the Word made a spotless sacrifice and oblation of the body he had taken. By dying for others, he immediately banished death for all mankind.

In this way the Word of God, who is above all, dedicated and offered his temple, the instrument that was his body, for us all, as he said, and so paid by his own death the debt that was owed. The immortal Son of God, united with all men by likeness of nature, thus fulfilled all justice in restoring mankind to immortality by the promise of the Resurrection.

The corruption of death no longer holds any power over mankind, thanks to the Word, who has come to dwell among them through his one body.

MAY 0 1 2003

From a Discourse Against the Arians, by Saint Athanasius

An impress of Wisdom has been created in us and in all his works. Therefore, the true Wisdom which shaped the world claims for himself all that bears his image, and rightly says: "The Lord created me in his works." These words are really spoken by the wisdom that is in us, but the Lord himself here adopts them as this own. Wisdom himself is not created, because he is the Creator, but by reason of the created image of himself found in his works, he speaks thus as though he were speaking of himself.

Our Lord said, "He who receives you receives me," and he could say this because the impress of himself is in us. In the same way, although Wisdom is not to be numbered among created things, yet because his form and likeness are in his works, he speaks as if he were a creature, and he says: "The Lord created me in his works, when his purpose first unfolded."

The likeness of Wisdom has been stamped upon creatures in order that the world may recognize in it the Word who was its maker and through the Word come to know the Father. This is Paul's teaching: "What can be known about God is clear to them, for God has shown it to them. Ever since the creation of the world his invisible nature has been there for the mind to perceive in things that have been made." Accordingly the Word is not a creature, for the passage that began: "The Lord created me" ... is to be understood as referring to that wisdom which is truly in us and is said to be so.

But if this fails to persuade our opponents, let them tell us whether there is any wisdom in created things. If there is none, why does the Apostle Paul allege as the cause of men's sins: "By God's wisdom, the world failed to come to a knowledge of God through wisdom"? And if there is no created wisdom, how is it that the expression "a multitude of wise men" is found in Scripture? And again, Scripture testifies that "the wise man is wary and turns away from evil," and "by wisdom is a house built." Further, Ecclesiastes says: "A wise man's wisdom will light up his face." He also rebukes presumptuous persons with the warning: "Do not say, 'How is it that former days were better than these?' For it is not in wisdom that you ask this."

So there is a wisdom in created things, as the son of Sirach too bears witness: "The Lord has poured it out upon all his works, to be with men as his gift, and with wisdom he has abundantly equipped those who love him." This quality of being "poured out" belongs not to the essence of that self-existent Wisdom who is the Only-begotten, but to that wisdom which reflects the Only-begotten one in the world.

Why then is it beyond belief if the creative and archetypal Wisdom, whose likeness is the wisdom and understanding poured out in the world, should say, as though speaking directly of himself: "The Lord created me in his works"? For the wisdom in the world is not creative, but is itself created in God's works, and in the light of this wisdom "the heavens declare the glory of God," and "the firmament proclaims the work of his hands."

From *The Life of Saint Anthony*, by Saint Athanasius

When Anthony was about eighteen or twenty years old, his parents died, leaving him with an only sister. He cared for her as she was very young, and also looked after their home.

Not six months after his parents' death, as he was on his way to church for his usual visit, he began to think of how the apostles had left everything and followed the Savior, and also of those mentioned in the book of Acts who had sold their possessions and brought the apostles the money for distribution to the needy. He reflected too on the great hope stored up in heaven for such as these. This was all in his mind when, entering the church just as the Gospel was being read, he heard the Lord's words to the rich man: "If you want to be perfect, go and sell all you have and give the money to the poor — you will have riches in heaven. Then come and follow me."

It seemed to Anthony that it was God who had brought the saints to his mind and that the words of the Gospel had been spoken directly to him. Immediately he left the church and gave away to the villagers all the property he had inherited, about 200 acres of very beautiful and fertile land, so that it would cause no distraction to his sister and himself. He sold all his other possessions as well, giving to the poor the considerable sum of money he collected. However, to care for his sister he retained a few things.

The next time he went to church he heard the Lord say in the Gospel: "Do not be anxious about tomorrow." Without a moment's hesitation he went out and gave the poor all that he had left. He placed his sister in the care of some well-known and trustworthy virgins and arranged for her to be brought up in the convent. Then he gave himself up to the ascetic life, not far from his own home. He kept a careful watch over himself and practiced great austerity. He did manual work because he had heard the word: "If anyone will not work, do not let him eat." He spent some of his earnings on bread and the rest he gave to the poor.

Having learned that we should always be praying, even when we are by ourselves, he prayed without ceasing. Indeed, he was so attentive when Scripture was read that nothing escaped him and because he retained all he heard, his memory served him in place of books.

Seeing the kind of life he lived, the villagers and all the good men he knew called him the friend of God, and they loved him as both son and brother.

CHAPTER 2

SAINT EPHREM

Of all the Doctors of the Church, it's probably fair to say that Saint Ephrem is the least known. This probably would please him because he was an exceptionally humble man. It also took the Church a long time to recognize Ephrem's teaching officially because, although he lived in the fourth century, he wasn't declared a Doctor of the Church until the twentieth century — in 1920, 1547 years after his death, by far the longest interval for any of the Doctors of the Church.

Although Ephrem wasn't declared a Doctor until 1920, the Church has always recognized him as a great poet, composer of hymns, orator, teacher, biblical exegete, theologian, and defender of the faith. Living and teaching, as he did, during the same century as Athanasius, Hilary, Cyril of Jerusalem, Basil the Great, Gregory Nazianzen, John Chrysostom, and Ambrose, Ephrem was deeply involved in combating the numerous false doctrines that sprang up, especially those concerning the Trinity, the Incarnation, and the Redemption.

Ephrem was born in or about the year 306 in Nisibis, Mesopotamia, which was still under Roman rule at the time. Biographers are divided over whether his parents were Christians or pagans but, in any event, he was baptized a Christian about the age of eighteen. The bishop of Nisibis at the time was a famous man now known as Saint Jacob, and Ephrem apparently became his follower. He is reported to have accompanied Bishop Jacob to the Council of Nicaea in 325 although this, too, is debated by scholars. After Bishop Jacob's death, Ephrem served the three succeeding bishops.

Soon Ephrem became well known as a superb teacher in the Christian biblical school of Nisibis. He was still in Nisibis when that city was attacked by the Persians, not only once but three times, and Ephrem was credited with securing the deliverance of the city by prayer in 328. Some of the hymns Ephrem wrote describe the Persians' attack, the city's defense, and the ultimate defeat of the enemy in 350. Unfortunately, after the city was successfully defended, it was given to the Persians thirteen years later during negotiations by the Persians and Roman Emperor Jovian.

After Nisibis was ceded to the Persians, Ephrem fled the city, along with many other Christians, to Edessa, where he taught theology. He found a cave in a rocky hill overlooking the city and moved into it. There he led an austere life, eating only bread and a few vegetables. It was here, too, that he wrote most of his spiritual works. According to the fifth-century Byzantine historian Sozomen, Ephrem wrote more than a thousand works during his lifetime.

Ephrem looked like the ascetic he was. He has been described as short in stature, bald, beardless, and with skin shriveled and dried up. His clothes consisted mainly of patches.

Ephrem seems to be among the first Christians to make sacred songs a part of public worship, although his contemporary Ambrose did so also. As one way to combat the heresies of his day, he took popular songs and, using their melodies, substituted texts embodying orthodox doctrines. His themes included the superiority of the virgin state of life, faith, and the existence of the Church as a continuation of Christ on earth. He trained a women's choir to sing the hymns during public worship. His hymns earned him the title "Harp of the Holy Spirit."

His writings, on dogmatic, exegetical, and ascetical subjects, show deep insight as well as a thorough knowledge of Scripture. He wrote commentaries on the Old Testament books of Genesis and Exodus, and he annotated the *Diatessaron*, a harmony of the Gospels drawn up by Tatian in the second century which became the standard Gospel text in the Syriac-speaking Churches until the fifth century. In writing about the Redemption, he demonstrated a great devotion to the humanity of Christ and he particularly revered the Virgin Mary for her sinless state. It is said that one of his poetical descriptions of heaven and hell influenced Dante when he wrote his *Divine Comedy*. Ephrem's works were translated from Syrian into Greek, Latin, and Armenian.

About the year 370, Ephrem traveled from Edessa to Caesarea in Cappadocia in order to visit Basil the Great, who had established a reputation for learning and holiness.

Ephrem's deep humility was exemplified by the fact that he never considered himself worthy to be ordained a priest and reportedly once prevented his being made a bishop by pretending to be insane. He was, however, ordained a deacon and he is often designated as Ephrem the Deacon. In that capacity, he administered large sums of money for the Church in Edessa. During the winter of 372, a famine caused considerable suffering among the people of Syria and Ephrem organized a relief operation which included providing 300 litters for carrying the sick.

Perhaps he overexerted himself performing that work because, after he returned to his cave overlooking the city, he died a month later, in 373.

The Church celebrates his feast on June 9.

From the Testament of Saint Ephrem

Lay me not with sweet spices,
For this honor avails me not,
Nor yet use incense and perfumes,
For the honor befits me not.
Burn yet the incense in the holy place;
As for me, escort me only with your prayers,
Give ye your incense to God,
And over me send up hymns.
Instead of perfumes and spices,
Be mindful of me in your intercessions.

From a Commentary on the *Diatessaron*, by Saint Ephrem

To prevent his disciples from asking the time of his coming, Christ said: "About that hour no one knows, neither the angels nor the Son. It is not for you to know times or moments." He has kept those things hidden so that we may keep watch, each of us thinking that he will come in our own day. If he had revealed the time of his coming, his coming would have lost its savor: it would no longer be an object of yearning for the nations and the age in which it will be revealed. He promised that he would come but did not say when he would come, and so all generations and ages await him eagerly.

Though the Lord has established the signs of his coming, the time of their fulfillment has not been plainly revealed. These signs have come and gone with a multiplicity of change; more than that, they are still present. His final coming is like his first. As holy men and prophets waited for him, thinking that he would reveal himself in their own day, so today each of the faithful longs to welcome him in his own day, because Christ has not made plain the day of his coming.

He has not made it plain for this reason especially, that no one may think that he whose power and dominion rule all numbers and times is ruled by fate and time. He described the signs of his coming; how could what he has himself decided be hidden from him? Therefore, he used those words to increase respect for the signs of his coming, so that from that day forward all generations and ages might think that he would come again in their own day.

Keep watch; when the body is asleep nature takes control of us, and what is done is not done by our will but by force, by the impulse of nature. When deep listlessness takes possession of the soul, for example, faintheartedness or melancholy, the enemy overpowers it and makes it do what it does not will. The force of nature, the enemy of the soul, is in control.

When the Lord commanded us to be vigilant, he meant vigilance in both parts of man: in the body, against the tendency to sleep; in the soul, against lethargy and timidity. As Scripture says: "Wake up, you just," and, "I have risen, and am still with you"; and again, "Do not lose heart. Therefore, having this ministry, we do not lose heart."

From a Sermon by Saint Ephrem

Death trampled our Lord underfoot, but he in his turn treated death as a highroad for his own feet. He submitted to it, enduring it willingly, because by this means he would be able to destroy death in spite of itself. Death had its own way when our Lord went out from Jerusalem carrying his cross; but when by a loud cry from that cross he summoned the dead from the underworld, death was powerless to prevent it.

Death slew him by means of the body which he had assumed, but that same body proved to be the weapon with which he conquered death. Concealed beneath the cloak of his manhood, his godhead engaged death in combat; but in slaying our Lord, death itself was slain. It was able to kill natural human life, but was itself killed by the life that is above the nature of man.

Death could not devour our Lord unless he possessed a body, neither could hell swallow him up unless he bore our flesh; and so he came in

search of a chariot in which to ride to the underworld. This chariot was the body which he received from the Virgin; in it he invaded death's
fortress, broke open its strong-room and scattered
all its treasure.

At length he came upon Eve, the mother of
all the living. She was that vineyard whose enclo-
sure her own hands had enabled death to violate,
so that she could taste its fruit; thus the mother of
all the living became the source of death for every living creature. But in her stead Mary grew up,
a new vine in place of the old. Christ, the new life,
dwelt within her. When death, with its customary
impudence, came foraging for her mortal fruit, it
encountered its own destruction in the hidden life
that fruit contained. All unsuspecting, it swallowed
him up, and in so doing released life itself and set
free a multitude of men.

He who was also the carpenter's glorious son
set up his cross above death's all-consuming jaws,
and led the human race into the dwelling place of
life. Since a tree had brought about the downfall
of mankind, it was upon a tree that mankind
crossed over to the realm of life. Bitter was the
branch that had once been grafted upon that ancient tree, but sweet the young shoot that has now
been grafted in, the shoot in which we are meant
to recognize the Lord whom no creature can resist.

We give glory to you, Lord, who raised up

your cross to span the jaws of death like a bridge by which souls might pass from the region of the dead to the land of the living. We give glory to you who put on the body of a single mortal man and made it the source of life for every other mortal man. You are incontestably alive. Your murderers sowed your living body in the earth as farmers sow grain, but it sprang up and yielded an abundant harvest of men raised from the dead.

Come then, my brothers and sisters, let us offer our Lord the great and all-embracing sacrifice of our love, pouring out our treasury of hymns and prayers before him who offered his cross in sacrifice to God for the enrichment of us all.

From a Sermon by Saint Ephrem

Lord, shed upon our darkened souls the brilliant light of your wisdom so that we may be enlightened and serve you with renewed purity. Sunrise marks the hour for men to begin their toil, but in our souls, Lord, prepare a dwelling for the day that will never end. Grant that we may come to know the risen life and that nothing may distract us from the delights you offer. Through our unremitting zeal for you, Lord, set upon us the sign of your day that is not measured by the sun.

In your sacrament we daily embrace you and receive you into our bodies; make us worthy to experience the resurrection for which we hope. We have had your treasure hidden within us ever since we received baptismal grace; it grows ever richer at your sacramental table. Teach us to find our joy in your favor! Lord, we have within us your memorial, received at your spiritual table; let us possess it in its full reality when all things shall be made new.

We glimpse the beauty that is laid up for us when we gaze upon the spiritual beauty your immortal will now creates within our mortal selves.

Savior, your crucifixion marked the end of your mortal life; teach us to crucify ourselves and make way for our life in the Spirit. May your resurrection, Jesus, bring true greatness to our spiritual self and may your sacraments be the mirror wherein we may know that self.

Savior, your divine plan for the world is a mirror for the spiritual world; teach us to walk in that world as spiritual men.

Lord, do not deprive our souls of the spiritual vision of you nor our bodies of your warmth and sweetness. The mortality lurking in our bodies spreads corruption through us; may the spiritual waters of your love cleanse the effects of mortality from our hearts. Grant, Lord, that we may hasten to our true city and, like Moses on the mountaintop, possess it now in vision.

CHAPTER 3

SAINT HILARY OF POITIERS

In America today, the name Hilary (or Hillary) has become a woman's name, but it originally was a man's name. The Saint Hilary who is a Doctor of the Church is known as Hilary of Poitiers to distinguish him from two other Saints Hilary — Saint Hilary of Arles, who was archbishop of that French city in the fifth century, and the Saint Hilary who was pope from 461 to 468.

Our Saint Hilary was born in Poitiers, in western Gaul (modern France) about fifty miles southwest of Tours and 125 miles northeast of Bordeaux, probably in 315. His parents were wealthy pagans who were able to provide their son with an excellent education, especially in the Latin classics and even some training in Greek, to prepare him to write and speak eloquently in public life. Unfortunately for the modern reader, though, Hilary's excessive imitation of classical models sometimes gives his writing an artificial and stilted tone. His long and involved sentences are often difficult to follow intelligently, as we will see when we read excerpts from his writings.

Hilary's studies in philosophy, rather than confirming him in the paganism of his parents, led him away from it. His reading of the Bible led him to Christianity and he was baptized, probably when he was in his early thirties.

Hilary was married and had a daughter named Apra when the people of Poitiers chose him as their bishop in 350 or 353. He tried to decline this position but his humility only made the people more determined in their choice and he finally assented. The people's choice proved to be an excellent one and Hilary soon was attracting the attention of the whole Church. His first published writing after he became a bishop was a commentary on the Gospel of Saint Matthew.

But events in the Church soon propelled him in another direction and Hilary very quickly became the main defender in the West against Arianism. He has become known as "the Hammerer of the Arians" and "the Athanasius of the West."

As we saw in the chapter about Athanasius, the Arian heresy was condemned by the Council of Nicaea in 325. The condemnation, though, did not mean the end of the heresy. It soon spread throughout the Christian world, mainly because of the efforts of Bishop Eusebius of Nicomedia, a personal friend of Emperor Constantine. Eusebius held a milder form of Arianism and his followers were known as Semi-Arians.

After Constantine's death the empire was divided among his three sons. Constantius was emperor of the East from 337 to 350 and of both the East and West from 350 to 361. As we saw in the chapter about Athanasius, Constantius was determined to crush Athanasius and to impose Arianism on the empire. He forced most of the bishops to condemn Athanasius at the councils of Arles and Milan. Hilary, however, refused to do so and wrote his *First Book to Constantius* urging the emperor to restore peace to the Church.

Emperor Constantius called another council at Beziers in 356. At this council Bishop Saturninus of Arles spoke in favor of Arianism and few bishops had the courage to argue in favor of the position taken at the Council of Nicaea. Hilary did, though, condemning Arianism in no uncertain terms. Saturninus reported this to Constantius, who sent orders for Hilary to be sent into exile. He was escorted to Phrygia, in Asia Minor, by Julian, the imperial commander in Gaul who later became emperor.

Hilary remained in exile for four years and it was during those years that he composed his masterpiece, twelve "books" (really long chapters) of *De Trinitate (On the Trinity)*. It was a complete exposition of the orthodox doctrine about the Trinity: that, while there is only one God and one divine nature, that one God is three divine persons — the Father, the Son, and the Holy Spirit. Each of the persons is "consubstantial" with the others, that is, has the same divine nature as the others. In addition to explaining the orthodox position, he also spelled out all the varieties of heresies that had arisen against the divinity of Christ, and refuted them. Hilary is credited with being the first Latin writer to acquaint the Christians of the West with the theological speculations of the East.

While in exile, besides writing for the benefit of Western Christians, Hilary also tried to win back to orthodoxy some of the Semi-Arians of the East. In 359, Emperor Constantius called a council of Arian bishops at Seleucia in Isauria to try to neutralize the Council of Nicaea. Some Semi-Arians invited Hilary to attend, hoping that he would help them defeat those who adhered strictly to Arianism. Once again he argued on behalf of orthodox doctrine. He then traveled to Constantinople where he presented to the emperor a request, known as his *Second Book to Constantius*, to hold a public debate with Saturninus. By this time the Arians were tired of dealing with Hilary and requested Constantius to send him back to Gaul "because he was a trouble-maker here."

Hilary returned to Poitiers in 360, traveling through Illyricum (modern Yugoslavia) and northern Italy on the way. It was a veritable triumphal procession. He was welcomed back to his diocese with great enthusiasm. One of those who was glad to see him was his disciple, Martin, who was later to become bishop of Tours and is known today as Saint Martin of Tours.

Once back in his own diocese, Hilary felt that he had some unfinished business to attend to. In 361 he convoked a council of the bishops of Gaul. The council condemned Saturninus and removed him from the See of Arles, thereby eliminating the last traces of Arianism in Gaul. That same year Emperor Constantius died and was succeeded by Julian the Apostate, who was more interested in trying to bring paganism back to the empire than in defending Arianism.

The final stronghold for Arianism was in Milan, where the Arian bishop was Auxentius. In 364 Hilary traveled to Milan and engaged Auxentius in a public debate, getting Auxentius to confess Christ to be true God, of the same substance and divinity as the Father.

Hilary then settled down to a more peaceful life. He resumed his writing on the Scriptures, most notably a commentary on the Psalms for which he borrowed heavily from Origen. He also composed a Latin translation of Origen's commentary on the Book of Job, but that is no longer in existence.

Hilary died in Poitiers, probably in 386 although we are not certain of either the year nor the day. He was proclaimed a Doctor of the Church by Pope Pius IX in 1851. The Church celebrates his feast on January 13.

From *On the Trinity,* by Saint Hilary

Many people find the Lord's words obscure when he says: "I in the Father and the Father in me," and there is nothing blameworthy in this, for man's natural power to reason does not grasp the meaning of this statement. It does not seem possible that the very thing which is in another is at the same time outside of it, and, since those things which we are discussing cannot exist apart from themselves, and, if they are to preserve the number and position in which they are, it seems that they cannot mutually contain each other, so that he who contains something else within himself and remains in this position and always remains outside of it can likewise be always present within him whom he contains within himself.

Human knowledge will certainly never grasp these truths and a comparison drawn from human things does not afford any similarity to divine things, but what man cannot conceive is possible to God. In thus expressing myself on this subject I have not meant that, because God has spoken these words, his authority alone suffices to apprehend them. We should examine and seek to realize the significance of this declaration: "I in the Father and the Father *in* me," provided we shall grasp it such as it really is, in order that what is regarded as incompatible with the nature of things will be obtained by the wisdom of the divine truth.

And that we may penetrate more easily into the knowledge of this most difficult question we must first understand the Father and the Son according to the teaching of the divine Scriptures, in order that, when we have learned to know them and have become familiar with them, our words may become clearer.

The eternity of God transcends places, times, appearance, and whatever can be conceived by the human mind. He is outside of all things and within all things; he comprises all things and is comprised by none; he does not change either by increase or decrease, but is invisible, incomprehensible, complete, perfect, and eternal; he does not know anything from elsewhere, but he himself is sufficient unto himself to remain what he is.

This unbegotten One, therefore, brought forth the Son from himself before all time, not from any pre-existing matter, because all things are through the Son; nor from nothing, because the Son is from him; nor as an ordinary birth, because there is nothing changeable or empty in God; nor as a part that is divided, cut off, or extended, because God is incapable of suffering and incorporeal and these things are characteristic of suffering and the flesh, and according to the Apostle: "In Christ dwells all the fullness of the Godhead bodily."

But in an inconceivable and ineffable manner, before all time and ages, he gave birth to the only-begotten God from that which in him was unbegotten, and through his charity and power he bestowed upon his birth everything that God is, and thus from the unbegotten, perfect, and eternal Father there is the only-begotten, perfect, and eternal Son. But that which belongs to him because of the body that he assumed results from the eagerness of his good will for our salvation. For, since he as one born from God is invisible, incorporeal, and inconceivable, he has taken upon himself as much matter and abasement as we possessed the power to understand, perceive, and comprehend, adapting himself to our weakness rather than abandoning those things which belonged to his own nature.

He is, therefore, the perfect Son of the perfect Father, the only-begotten offspring of the unbegotten God, who has received everything from him who possesses everything. He is God from God, Spirit from Spirit, Light from Light, and he proclaims with assurance: "I in the Father and the Father in me." As the Father is Spirit, so the Son also is Spirit; as the Father is God, so the Son also is God; as the Father is Light so the Son also is Light. From those things, therefore, which are in the Father are also those things which are in the Son, that is, from the whole Father the whole Son is born; he is not from anywhere else, because nothing was before the Son; he is not from nothingness, because the Son is from God; he is not a

God in part only, because the fullness of the God-head is in the Son, not in some things because he is in all things, but as he willed who could, as he knows who begot him.

Whatever is in the Father is also in the Son; whatever is in the unbegotten is also in the only-begotten, one from the other and both are one substance, not one person, but one is in the other because there is nothing different in either of them. The Father is in the Son because the Son is from him; the Son in the Father because he is not a Son from anywhere else; the only-begotten is in the unbegotten because the only-begotten is from the unbegotten. Thus, they are mutually in each other, because as all things are perfect in the Father, so all things are perfect in the Son,

This is the unity in the Father and the Son, this is the power, this the charity, this the hope, this the faith, this the truth, the way, and the life, not to spread false reports about God concerning his attributes, nor to disparage the Son because of the mystery and power of his birth, not to place anything on an equality with the unbegotten Father, nor to separate the only-begotten from him in time or power, but to acknowledge him as the Son of God because he is from God.

* * *

We believe that the Word became flesh and that we receive his flesh in the Lord's Supper. How then can we fail to believe that he really dwells within us? When he became man, he actually clothed himself in our flesh, uniting it to himself forever. In the sacrament of his body he actually gives us his own flesh, which he has united to his divinity. This is why we are all one, because the Father is in Christ, and Christ is in us. He is in us through his flesh and we are in him. With him we form a unity which is in God.

The manner of our indwelling in him through the sacrament of his body and blood is evident from the Lord's own words: "This world will see me no longer but you shall see me. Because I live you shall live also, for I am in my Father, you are in me, and I am in you." If it had been a question of a mere unity of will, why should he have given us this explanation of the steps by which it is achieved? He is in the Father by reason of his divine nature, we are in him by reason of his human birth, and he is in us through the mystery of the sacraments. This, surely, is what he wished us to believe; this is how he wanted us to understand the perfect unity that is achieved through our Mediator, who lives in the Father while we live in him, and who, while living in the Father, lives also in us. This is how we attain to unity with the Father. Christ is in very truth in the Father by his eternal generation; we are in very truth in Christ, and he likewise is in us.

Christ himself bore witness to the reality of

this unity when he said: "He who eats my flesh and drinks my blood lives in me and I in him." No one will be in Christ unless Christ himself has been in him; Christ will take to himself only the flesh of those who have received his flesh.

He had already explained the mystery of this perfect unity when he said: "As the living Father sent me and I draw life from the Father, so he who eats my flesh will draw life from me." We draw life from his flesh just as he draws life from the Father. Such comparisons aid our understanding, since we can grasp a point more easily when we have an analogy. And the point is that Christ is the wellspring of our life. Since we who are in the flesh have Christ dwelling in us through his flesh, we shall draw life from him in the same way as he draws life from the Father.

From a Commentary on Psalm 128, by Saint Hilary

"Blessed are those who fear the Lord, who walk in his way." Notice that when Scripture speaks of the fear of the Lord it does not leave the phrase in isolation, as if it were a complete summary of faith. No, many things are added to it, or are presupposed by it. From these we may learn its meaning and excellence. In the Book of Proverbs Solomon tells us: "If you cry out for wisdom and raise your voice for understanding, if you look for it as for silver and search for it as for treasure, then you will understand the fear of the Lord." We see here the difficult journey we must undertake before we can arrive at the fear of the Lord.

We must begin by crying out for wisdom. We must hand over to our intellect the duty of making every decision. We must look for wisdom and search for it. Then we must understand the fear of the Lord.

"Fear" is not to be taken in the sense that common usage gives it. Fear in this ordinary sense is the trepidation our weak humanity feels when it is afraid of suffering something it does not want to happen. We are afraid, or are made afraid, because of a guilty conscience, the rights of someone more powerful, an attack from one who is stronger, sickness, encountering a wild beast, suffering evil in any form. This kind of fear is not taught: it happens because we are weak. We do not have to learn what we should fear: objects of fear bring their own terror with them.

But of the fear of the Lord this is what is written: "Come, my children, listen to me; I shall teach you the fear of the Lord." The fear of the Lord has then to be learned because it can be taught. It does not lie in terror, but in something that can be taught. It does not arise from the fearfulness of our nature; it has to be acquired by obedience to the commandments, by holiness of life and by knowledge of the truth.

For us the fear of God consists wholly in love, and perfect love of God brings our fear of him to its perfection. Our love for God is entrusted with its own responsibility: to observe his counsels, to obey his laws, to trust his promises. Let us hear what Scripture says: "And now, Israel, what does the Lord your God ask of you except to fear the Lord your God and walk in all his ways and love him and keep his commandments with your whole heart and your whole soul, so that it may be well for you?"

The ways of the Lord are many, though he is himself the way. When he speaks of himself he calls himself the way and shows us the reason why he called himself the way: "No one can come to the Father except through me." We must ask for these many ways, we must travel along these many ways, to find the one that is good. That is, we shall find the one way of eternal life through the guidance of many teachers. These ways are found in the law, in the prophets, in the gospels, in the writings of the apostles, in the different good works by which we fulfill the commandments. Blessed are those who walk these ways in the fear of the Lord.

CHAPTER 4

SAINT CYRIL OF JERUSALEM

It might be difficult for us in the twentieth century to fully understand the seriousness of the heresy of Arianism during the fourth century. But all six of the earliest Doctors of the Church were involved in one way or another with that heresy. Cyril of Jerusalem, though, is unique in that he is certainly the only Doctor who was accused of being an Arian. This accusation came from Saint Jerome. However, the First Council of Constantinople praised Cyril as a champion of orthodoxy against the Arians. Cyril, obviously, was often in the middle of controversy.

Although he was not friendly with the greatest champion against Arianism, Athanasius, Cyril and Athanasius had one thing in common — both lived much of their lives exiled from their dioceses. Of his 35 years as bishop, Cyril was in exile for 16 of them.

He was born in Jerusalem about the year 315. However, at the time Jerusalem was known as Aelia Capitolina, the name given the city by the Romans after they destroyed the city for the second time in 135. Cyril's parents were Christians and were sufficiently wealthy to be able to afford a good education for him, especially in the Scriptures. He was ordained a priest by Bishop Maximus and given responsibility for teaching the catechumens the fundamentals of the faith before their baptism.

It has been reported that Cyril's instructions to the catechumens were delivered without a book. However, eighteen of his catechetical discourses for baptismal candidates during Lent, known as *Catecheses*, and five for the newly baptized after Easter, known as the *Mystagogic*, have come down to us. They are valuable because they tell us about the ritual and theology of the Church in the early fourth century. It was mainly these works that earned Cyril the designation as a Doctor of the Church.

When Cyril was growing up Jerusalem was not considered an important diocese. After the city was destroyed by the Romans, it was rebuilt, renamed Aelia Capitolina, and dedicated to the Roman gods Jupiter, Juno, and Minerva. Caesarea, on the Mediterranean coast, became far more important to the small group of Christians then living in the Holy Land, and the Church in Aelia was subordinate to the Church in Caesarea. All that began to change, though, after Constantine legalized the practice of Christianity, and particularly beginning in 326 when Helena, Constantine's mother, visited the Holy Land. She began building the Church of the Holy Sepulchre and the Church of the Ascension in Jerusalem, and the Church of the Nativity in nearby Bethlehem.

That was the situation, then, when Cyril became bishop of Jerusalem in 349 or 350, succeeding Bishop Maximus. Cyril led efforts to make Jerusalem a place of pilgrimage, emphasizing that the most momentous events in Christian salvation history happened in Jerusalem — including, of course, Christ's crucifixion and death, his resurrection, and the descent of the Holy Spirit. He claimed that the descent of the Holy Spirit gave Jerusalem "preeminence in all things," and he campaigned for recognition of the Church in Jerusalem as the primary Church in Palestine.

This tended to inflame a controversy that already existed between the Churches in Jerusalem and Caesarea, since the bishops of Caesarea were Arians — first Eusebius and then Acacius. Finally, in 357, Acacius called a council of Arian bishops and ordered Cyril to appear to defend himself against charges of insubordination and the selling of Church property during a famine to relieve the poor. He indeed had sold Church property for that purpose. Cyril refused to appear before the council, which condemned him and drove him out of Jerusalem — his first exile.

Cyril made his way to Tarsus, where the Semi-Arian bishop there, Silvanus, was hospitable.

He remained there for two years awaiting an appeal which he had sent to a higher court. That appeal came before the Council of Seleucia, the same council that heard Hilary of Poitiers defend himself. Most of the bishops at the council were Semi-Arians or hard-core Arians, with only a few members of the strictly orthodox party. Cyril had been befriended by Semi-Arian bishops and he sat with them during the council's proceedings, and it was this that was later to lead to accusations that he shared Arian beliefs.

Bishop Acacius of Caesarea was angered that Cyril was present at the council, and he stormed out — although he returned later to participate in the proceedings. In this case, though, Cyril had more friends than Acacius; Cyril was reinstated in his diocese while Acacius was deposed from his. Cyril returned to Jerusalem.

He was there for less than a year. Acacius persuaded Emperor Constantius to convene another council, dominated by Arians, and this time Cyril was deposed a second time. But Constantius died in 361 and his successor Julian recalled all the bishops Constantius had exiled, including Cyril in Jerusalem and Athanasius in Alexandria. Julian was later to exile Athanasius again, but Cyril survived that reign without banishment.

Cyril's last exile came in 367 when Emperor Valens decreed the expulsion of all prelates recalled by Julian. He returned to Jerusalem after

Valens was defeated and killed in the Battle of Adrianople in 378. He then was able to remain in his see for the last eight years of his episcopacy.

When he returned, though, he found Jerusalem to be in a state of severe moral decay, torn by schisms, heresy, and appalling crimes. He asked the Council of Antioch for help and that council sent Gregory of Nyssa (Saint Basil's brother) to see what he could do, but Gregory soon left in despair. Cyril was left to try to bring reforms to his city.

The second ecumenical council, the First Council of Constantinople, was held in 381, and Cyril attended. He took his place as a metropolitan with the patriarchs of Alexandria and Antioch. This was the council that amended and approved the Nicene Creed that Catholics recite at Sunday Masses today. Prior to the council, Cyril was known to oppose the term *Homoousios*, the Greek word for "consubstantial," to affirm the full divinity of God the Son as he shares the divine substance of the Father. Cyril considered the word to be "manmade." However, at the council he accepted the term along with the other council Fathers. This term came to be regarded as the test word of orthodoxy. At the council, Cyril was praised as a champion of orthodoxy against the Arians.

Cyril died in Jerusalem in 386, about the age of 71. He was declared a Doctor of the Church by Pope Leo XIII in 1882. The Church celebrates his feast on March 18.

Excerpts from *Catecheses*,
by Saint Cyril of Jerusalem

The Church is called Catholic or universal because it has spread throughout the entire world, from one end of the earth to the other. Again, it is called Catholic because it teaches fully and unfailingly all the doctrines which ought to be brought to men's knowledge, whether concerned with visible or invisible things, with the realities of heaven or the things of earth.

Another reason for the name Catholic is that the Church brings under religious obedience all classes of men, rulers and subjects, learned and unlettered. Finally, it deserves the title Catholic because it heals and cures unrestrictedly every type of sin that can be committed in soul or in body, and because it possesses within itself every kind of virtue that can be named, whether exercised in actions or in words or in some kind of spiritual charism.

It is most aptly called a church, which means an "assembly of those called out," because it "calls out" all men and gathers them together, just as the Lord says in Leviticus: "Assemble all the congregation at the door of the tent of meeting." It is worth noting also that the word "assemble" is used for the first time in the Scriptures at this moment when the Lord appoints Aaron high priest. So in Deuteronomy God says to Moses: "Assemble the people before me and let them hear my words, so that they may learn to fear me."

There is a further mention of the assembly in the passage about the tablets of the Law: "And on them were written all the words which the Lord had spoken to you on the mountain out of the midst of the fire, on the day of the assembly"; it is as though he had said, even more clearly, "on the day when you were called out by God and gathered together." So too the psalmist says: "I will give thanks to you in the great assembly, O Lord; in the mighty throng I will praise you."

Long ago the psalmist sang: "Bless God in the assembly; bless the Lord, you who are Israel's sons." But now the Savior has built a second holy assembly, our Christian Church, from the Gentiles. It was of this that he spoke to Peter: "On this rock I will build my Church, and the powers of death shall not prevail against it."

Now that the single church which was in Judea has been rejected, the churches of Christ are already multiplying throughout the world, and of them it is said in the psalms: "Sing a new song to the Lord, let his praise be sung in the assembly of the saints." Taking up the same theme the prophet says to the Jews: "I have no pleasure in you, says the Lord of hosts"; and immediately he adds: "For from the rising of the sun to its setting my name is glorified among the nations."

Of this holy Catholic Church Paul writes to

Timothy: "That you may know how one ought to behave in the household of God, which is the Church of the living God, the pillar and bulwark of the truth."

MAR 1 8 2003   * * *

The Catholic Church glories in every deed of Christ. Her supreme glory, however, is the cross. Well aware of this, Paul says: "God forbid that I glory in anything but the cross of our Lord Jesus Christ!"

At Siloam, there was a sense of wonder, and rightly so. A man born blind recovered his sight. But of what importance is this, when there are so many blind people in the world? Lazarus rose from the dead, but even this only affected Lazarus. What of those countless numbers who have died because of their sins? Those five miraculous loaves fed five thousand people. Yet this is a small number compared to those all over the world who were starved by ignorance. After eighteen years a woman was freed from the bondage of Satan. But are we not all shackled by the chains of our own sins?

For us all, however, the cross is the crown of victory! It has brought light to those blinded by ignorance. It has released those enslaved by sin. Indeed, it has redeemed the whole of mankind!

Do not, then, be ashamed of the cross of Christ; rather, glory in it. Although it is a stumbling block to the Jews and folly to the Gentiles, the message of the cross is our salvation. Of course it is folly to those who are perishing, but to us who are being saved it is the power of God. For it was not a mere man who died for us, but the Son of God, God-made-man.

In the Mosaic Law, a sacrificial lamb banished the destroyer. But now "it is the Lamb of God who takes away the sin of the world." Will he not free us from our sins even more? The blood of an animal, a sheep, brought salvation. Will not the blood of the only-begotten Son bring us greater salvation?

He was not killed by violence, he was not forced to give up his life. His was a willing sacrifice. Listen to his own words: "I have the power to lay down my life and to take it up again." Yes, he willingly submitted to his own passion. He took joy in his achievement; in his crown of victory he was glad and in the salvation of man he rejoiced. He did not blush at the cross for by it he was to save the world. No, it was not a lowly man who suffered, but God incarnate. He entered the contest for the reward he would win by his patient endurance.

Certainly in times of tranquillity the cross should give you joy. But maintain the same faith in times of persecution. Otherwise you will be a friend of Jesus in times of peace and his enemy during war. Now you receive the forgiveness of your sins and the generous gift of grace from your king. When war comes, fight courageously for him.

Jesus never sinned; yet he was crucified for you. Will you refuse to be crucified for him, who for your sake was nailed to the cross? You are not the one who gives the favor; you have received one first. For your sake he was crucified on Golgotha. Now you are returning his favor; you are fulfilling your debt to him.

* * *

The one word faith can have two meanings. One kind of faith concerns doctrines. It involves the soul's ascent to and acceptance of some particular matter. It also concerns the soul's good, according to the words of the Lord: "Whoever hears my voice and believes in him who sent me has eternal life, and will not come to be judged." And again: "He who believes in the Son is not condemned, but has passed from death to life."

How great is God's love for men! Some good men have been found pleasing to God because of years of work. What they achieved by working for many hours at a task pleasing to God is freely given to you by Jesus in one short hour. For if you believe that Jesus Christ is Lord and that God raised him from the dead, you will be saved and taken up to paradise by him, just as he brought the thief there. Do not doubt that this is possible. After all, he saved the thief on the holy hill of Golgotha because of one hour's faith; will he not save you too since you have believed?

The other kind of faith is given by Christ by means of a special grace. "To one wise sayings are given through the Spirit, to another perceptive comments by the same Spirit, to another faith by the same Spirit, to another gifts of healing." Now this kind of faith, given by the Spirit as a special favor, is not confined to doctrinal matters, for it produces effects beyond any human capability. If a man who has this faith says to this mountain, "Move from here to there, it will move." For when anybody says this in faith, believing it will happen and having no doubt in his heart, he then receives that grace.

It is of this kind of faith, moreover, that it is said: "If you have faith like a grain of mustard seed." The mustard seed is small in size but it holds an explosive force; although it is sown in a small hole, it produces great branches, and when it is grown birds can nest there. In the same way faith produces great effects in the soul instantaneously. Enlightened by faith, the soul pictures God and sees him as clearly as any soul can. It circles the earth; even before the end of this world it sees the judgment and the conferring of promised rewards. So may you have the faith which depends on you and is directed to God, that you may receive from him that faith too which transcends man's capacity.

In learning and professing the faith, you must accept and retain only the Church's present tradition, confirmed as it is by the Scriptures. Although not everyone is able to read the Scriptures, some because they have never learned to read, others because their daily activities keep them from such study, still so that their souls will not be lost through ignorance, we have gathered together the whole of the faith in a few concise articles.

Now I order you to retain this creed for your nourishment throughout life and never to accept any alternative, not even if I myself were to change and say something contrary to what I am now teaching, not even if some angel of contradiction, changed into an angel of light, tried to lead you astray. For [as Saint Paul wrote], "Even if we, or an angel from heaven, should preach to you a gospel contrary to that which you have [now] received, let him be accursed in your sight."

So for the present be content to listen to the simple words of the creed and to memorize them; at some suitable time you can find the proof of each article in the Scriptures. This summary of the faith was not composed at man's whim; the most important sections were chosen from the whole Scripture to constitute and complete a comprehensive statement of the faith. Just as the mustard seed contains in a small grain many branches, so this brief statement of the faith keeps in its heart, as it were, all the religious truth to be found in Old and

New Testament alike. That is why, my brothers, you must consider and preserve the traditions you are now receiving. Inscribe them across your heart.

Observe them scrupulously, so that no enemy may rob any of you in an idle and heedless moment; let no heretic deprive you of what has been given to you. Faith is rather like depositing in a bank the money entrusted to you, and God will surely demand an account of what you have deposited. In the words of the Apostle: "I charge you before the God who gives life to all things, and before Christ who bore witness under Pontius Pilate in a splendid declaration," to keep unblemished this faith you have received, until the coming of our Lord Jesus Christ.

You have now been given life's great treasure; when he comes the Lord will ask for what he has entrusted to you. "At the appointed time he will reveal himself, for he is the blessed and sole Ruler, King of kings, Lord of lords. He alone is immortal, dwelling in unapproachable light. No man has seen or ever can see him." To him be glory, honor and power for ever and ever. Amen.

CHAPTER 5

SAINT BASIL THE GREAT

Four of the Doctors of the Church have the honorific title "the Great" added to their names: Basil, Pope Leo, Pope Gregory, and Albert. Basil, though, was already being called "the Great" during his lifetime, so "great" were his accomplishments. These included leaving his mark for all times on the formation of Eastern monasticism and the liturgy of the Eastern Church, and becoming the principal defender of orthodox Christianity in the East against Arianism after the death of Athanasius. As Hilary was defending Church doctrine in the West, Basil was doing so in the East.

Basil was born in Caesarea of Cappadocia towards the end of the year 329. This was not the Caesarea in Palestine (present-day Israel) that, as we saw in the previous chapter, was under the control of Arian bishops and which was a rival to Jerusalem when Cyril was bishop of the latter city. Nor was it the Caesarea Philippi in the present-day Golan Heights where Jesus conferred the "keys of the kingdom" on Peter. Caesarea of Cappadocia was situated in eastern Asia Minor, now Turkey.

Basil was quite literally born into a family of saints. One of his great-grandfathers died as a martyr. The Church venerates his grandmother as Saint Macrina the Elder and both of his parents — Basil the Elder and Emmelia — are saints. His brother was Saint Gregory of Nyssa and one of his sisters (his parents had ten children) is known as Saint Macrina the Younger.

Basil the Elder was a Christian lawyer who had suffered persecution and exile for his faith, and he died when his namesake son was young. Basil's mother reared her children in a model Christian home and Basil wrote that his grandmother, Saint Macrina the Elder, gave him early lessons in Christianity.

Basil was highly educated, first in Caesarea, then in Constantinople, the capital of the empire, and finally in Athens, Greece. In Athens it happened that one of his classmates was Julian, later to become known as Emperor Julian the Apostate because of his efforts to return the empire to paganism. Neither man, though, seems to have been an influence on the other.

Basil's closest friend in Athens was another man from Cappadocia, Gregory, who was later to become bishop of Nazianzus and, like Basil, a Doctor of the Church. As Gregory was later to write, "We seemed to be two bodies with a single spirit." (An excerpt from Gregory's description of their years together in Athens is included with

Gregory's writings in the next chapter.) Basil, Gregory of Nazianzus, and Basil's brother, Gregory of Nyssa, were later to become known as "the three Cappadocians" as they all distinguished themselves in their service to the Church.

After his education in Athens, Basil returned to Caesarea in 356, when he was about twenty-six. In accordance with the custom at that time of delaying baptism until a person was mature, he was baptized by Danius, the bishop of Caesarea. Basil had undergone a conversion and was determined to devote the rest of his life to God. Accordingly, he began a two-year journey to visit the various places in Asia Minor, Mesopotamia, Syria, and Palestine where men lived as hermits, most of them following the example of Saint Anthony of Egypt. They lived far from the distractions of cities, spending their time in prayer and penance.

Although Basil greatly admired these hermits, he believed that it would be better, both for them and for their fellow Christians, if they would join their cells together to form one monastery or *laura*. They could continue to live lives of prayer and penance, but they would also have the spiritual advantage of practicing obedience to an abbot who would guide them. The abbot would also make sure that the hermits' manual labor or their work in libraries or classrooms would be beneficial to their fellow Christians.

On his return from his trip in 359, therefore,

Basil decided to establish the first monastery of this kind and he invited his friend Gregory to join him. Gregory was glad to accept. It happened that his mother and sister Macrina had already founded a convent for nuns on property they owned on the bank of the River Iris in Pontus. Basil found property on the other side of the river and set up his monastery there. Soon other men joined Basil and Gregory and, within a few years, several other monasteries were established.

For the benefit of these monasteries, Basil wrote a series of "Rules." They weren't strict precepts for what is necessary for monasteries, but more in the nature of exhortations. They formed the basis for what is known as the Rule of Saint Basil upon which all monasteries of Eastern Christianity are based, including those of modern Orthodox Churches. Thus Basil is known as "the Father of Eastern Monasticism," just as Saint Benedict of Nursia is called "the Father of Western Monasticism." At least indirectly, Basil influenced all the numerous orders and congregations of religious men and women.

Basil was content in his monastery, but the religious controversies of his day forced him to become involved in defending Christianity against Arianism. He was convinced to attend a regional council at Constantinople in 360. In 363, he consented to be ordained a priest and he immediately began to play an important role in the administration of the diocese, so much so that he got into a dispute with his bishop and returned to his monastery. He was recalled in 365, though, at the insistence of Gregory of Nazianzus, and was the power behind the episcopal throne for the next five years. When the bishop died in 370 Basil was chosen bishop of Caesarea, and spent the next eight-and-a-half years caring for the spiritual and temporal welfare of his flock.

Basil was known for his care of the poor, devoting all of his income to the good of the people. He founded an immense charitable institution, later known as the Basilade, which included a hospital that was called a wonder of the world. It included a hospice for the homeless, an asylum for orphans, and a school for the young.

He preached brilliant sermons twice a day, and some of those sermons have come down to us: nine on the creation of the world, nine more on the Psalms, and twenty-four on various other religious topics. His writings include the book *On the Holy Spirit*; three books against Enomius, an outspoken Arian bishop; and a compilation with Gregory of Nazianzus of the works of Origen. It was his sermons, his writings, and some 366 letters that earned his designation as a Doctor of the Church.

Basil was also involved in reforming Eastern Christianity's liturgy. One of the forms in which the Mass is celebrated in the Greek Orthodox

Church is still called "the Liturgy of Saint Basil."

In his battle against Arianism, Basil had to face Emperor Valens, who did all he could to force Basil to subscribe to Arianism. Valens sent the imperial "prefect" or chief of police, a man named Modestus, to threaten Basil with torture and exile if he didn't espouse Arianism. But Basil stood his ground, replying that the threats of banishment meant nothing to him since he was already an exile from heaven and no place on earth was really his home. As for torture, he said that he already suffered from a chest ailment and was sure that, with the first few lashes of the scourge, he would leave this world to be with Christ — a thing he ardently longed for.

That chest pain and other infirmities brought about his death on January 1, 379, at age 49. Because he was so beloved, his funeral was attended by a large number of Christians, Jews and pagans. He was always honored by the Church as a great saint and theologian. Seventy-two years after his death the Council of Chalcedon described him as "the great Basil, minister of grace who has expounded the truth to the whole earth."

The Church celebrates his feast, along with that of Gregory of Nazianzus, on January 2.

From *Detailed Rules for Monks,* by Saint Basil

Love of God is not something that can be taught. We did not learn from someone else how to rejoice in light or want to live, or to love our parents or guardians. It is the same — perhaps even more so — with our love for God: it does not come by another's teaching. As soon as the living creature (that is, man) comes to be, a power of reason is implanted in us like a seed, containing within it the ability and the need to love. When the school of God's law admits this power of reason, it cultivates it diligently, skillfully nurtures it, and with God's help brings it to perfection.

For this reason, as by God's gift, I find you with the zeal necessary to attain this end, and you on your part help me with your prayers. I will try to fan into flame the spark of divine love that is hidden within you, as far as I am able through the power of the Holy Spirit.

First, let me say that we have already received from God the ability to fulfill all his commands. We have then no reason to resent them, as if something beyond our capacity were being asked of us. We have no reason either to be angry, as if we had to pay back more than we had received. When we use this ability in a right and fitting way, we lead a life of virtue and holiness. But if we misuse it, we fall into sin.

This is the definition of sin: the misuse of powers given us by God for doing good, a use contrary to God's commandments. On the other hand, the virtue that God asks of us is the use of the same powers based on a good conscience in accordance with God's command.

Since this is so, we can say the same about love. Since we received a command to love God, we possess from the first moment of our existence an innate power and ability to love. The proof of this is not to be sought outside ourselves, but each one can learn this from himself and in himself. It is natural for us to want things that are good and pleasing to the eye, even though at first different things seem beautiful and good to different people. In the same way, we love what is related to us or near to us, though we have not been taught to do so, and we spontaneously feel well disposed to our benefactors.

What, I ask, is more wonderful than the beauty of God? What thought is more pleasing and satisfying than God's majesty? What desire is as urgent and overpowering as the desire implanted by God in a soul that is completely purified of sin and cries out in its love: "I am wounded by love"? The radiance of the divine beauty is altogether beyond the power of words to describe.

From *On the Holy Spirit*, by Saint Basil

The titles given to the Holy Spirit must surely stir the soul of anyone who hears them, and make him realize that they speak of nothing less than the supreme Being. Is he not called the Spirit of God, the Spirit of truth who proceeds from the Father, the steadfast Spirit, the guiding Spirit? But his principal and most personal title is the Holy Spirit.

To the Spirit all creatures turn in their need for sanctification; all living things seek him according to their ability. His breath empowers each to achieve its own natural end.

The Spirit is the source of holiness, a spiritual light, and he offers his own light to every mind to help it in its search for truth. By nature the Spirit is beyond the reach of our mind, but we can know him by his goodness. The power of the Spirit fills the whole universe, but he gives himself only to those who are worthy, acting in each according to the measure of his faith.

Simple in himself, the Spirit is manifold in his mighty works. The whole of his being is present to each individual; the whole of his being is present everywhere. Though shared in by many, he remains unchanged; his self-giving is no loss to himself. Like the sunshine, which permeates all the atmosphere, spreading over land and sea, and yet is enjoyed by each person as though it were for him alone, so the Spirit pours forth his grace in full measure, sufficient for all, and yet is present as though exclusively to everyone who can receive him. To all creatures that share in him he gives a delight limited only by their own nature, not by his ability to give.

The Spirit raises our hearts to heaven, guides the steps of the weak, and brings to perfection those who are making progress. He enlightens those who have been cleansed from every stain of sin and makes them spiritual by communion with himself.

As clear, transparent substances become very bright when sunlight falls on them and shine with a new radiance, so also souls in whom the Spirit dwells, and who are enlightened by the Spirit, become spiritual themselves and a source of grace for others.

From the Spirit comes foreknowledge of the future, understanding of the mysteries of faith, insight into the hidden meaning of Scripture, and other special gifts. Through the Spirit we become citizens of heaven, we are admitted to the company of the angels, we enter into eternal happiness, and abide in God. Through the Spirit we acquire a likeness to God; indeed, we attain what is beyond our most sublime aspirations — we become God.

From a Sermon on Charity, by Saint Basil

Man should be like the earth and bear fruit; he should not let inanimate matter appear to surpass him. The earth bears crops for your benefit, not for its own, but when you give to the poor, you are bearing fruit which you will gather in for yourself, since the reward for good deeds goes to those who perform them. Give to the hungry man, and what you give becomes yours, and indeed it returns to you with interest. As the sower profits from wheat that falls onto the ground, so will you profit greatly in the world to come from the bread that you place before a hungry man. Your husbandry must be the sowing of heavenly seed: "Sow integrity for yourselves," says Scripture.

You are going to leave your money behind you here whether you wish to or not. On the other hand, you will take with you to the Lord the honor that you have won through good works. In the presence of the universal judge, all the people will surround you, acclaim you as a public benefactor, and tell of your generosity and kindness.

Do you not see how people throw away their wealth on theatrical performances, boxing contests, mimes, and fights between men and wild beasts, which are sickening to see, and all for the sake of fleeting honor and popular applause? If you are miserly with your money, how can you expect any similar honor? Your reward for the right use of the things of this world will be everlasting glory, a crown of righteousness, and the kingdom of heaven; God will welcome you, the angels will praise you, all men who have existed since the world began will call you blessed. Do you care nothing for these things, and spurn the hopes that lie in the future for the sake of your present enjoyment? Come, distribute your wealth freely, give generously to those who are in need. Earn for yourself the psalmist's praise: "He gave freely to the poor; his righteousness will endure forever."

How grateful you should be to your own benefactor; how you should beam with joy at the honor of having other people come to your door, instead of being obliged to go to theirs! But you are now ill-humored and unapproachable; you avoid meeting people, in case you might be forced to loosen your purse-strings even a little. You can say only one thing: "I have nothing to give you. I am only a poor man." A poor man you certainly are, and destitute of all real riches; you are poor in love, generosity, faith in God and hope of eternal happiness.

From a Homily on Humility, by Saint Basil

How shall we, casting off the deadly weight of pride, descend to saving humility? If such an aim governed our conduct under all circumstances, we should not overlook the least detail on the ground that we would suffer no harm therefrom. The soul comes to take on a resemblance to its preoccupations and it is stamped and molded to the form of its activities.

Let your aspect, your garb, your manner of walking and sitting, your diet, bed, house and its furnishings reflect a customary thrift. Your manner of speaking and singing, your conversation with your neighbor, also, should aim at modesty rather than pretentiousness. Do not strive, I beg you, for artificial embellishment in speech, for cloying sweetness in song, or for a sonorous and high-flown style in conversation.

In all your actions, be free from pomposity. Be obliging to your friends, gentle toward your slaves, forbearing with the forward, benign to the lowly, a source of comfort to the afflicted, a friend to the distressed, a condemner of no one. Be pleasant in your address, genial in your response, courteous, accessible to all. Do not listen to indecent talk, and conceal insofar as you can your own superior gifts.

On the other hand, where sin is concerned, be your own accuser, and do not wait for others to make the accusation. Thus, you will be like a just man who accuses himself in the first speech made in court, or like Job who was not deterred by the crowd of people in the city from declaring his personal guilt before all.

Be not rash in rebuking, nor quick to do so. Do not make accusations while your passions are aroused (for such action savors of willfulness), nor condemn anyone in matters of slight consequence as if you yourself were perfectly just. Receive those who have fallen away and give them spiritual instruction, "considering thyself also lest thou be tempted," as the Apostle advises.

Take as much care not to be glorified among men as others do to obtain this glory, as you remember the words of Christ, that one forfeits a reward from God by voluntarily seeking renown from men or do good to be seen by men. "They have received their reward," he says. Do not cheat yourself by desiring to be seen by men, for God is the great Witness. Strive for glory with God, for his is a glorious recompense.

From a Homily on Boasting, by Saint Basil

"The wise man must not boast of his wisdom, nor the strong man of his strength, nor the rich man of his riches." What then is the right kind of boasting? What is the source of man's greatness? Scripture says: "The man who boasts must boast of this, that he knows and understands that I am the Lord." Here is man's greatness, here is man's glory and majesty: to know in truth what is great, to hold fast to it, and to seek glory from the Lord of glory.

The Apostle tells us: "The man who boasts

must boast of the Lord." He has just said: "Christ was appointed by God to be our wisdom, our righteousness, our sanctification, our redemption, so that, as it is written, a man who boasts must boast of the Lord."

Boasting of God is perfect and complete when we take no pride in our own righteousness but acknowledge that we are utterly lacking in true righteousness and have been made righteous only by faith in Christ.

Paul boasts of the fact that he holds his own righteousness in contempt and seeks the righteousness in faith that comes through Christ and is from God. He wants only to know Christ and the power of his resurrection and to have fellowship with his sufferings by taking on the likeness of his death, in the hope that somehow he may arrive at the resurrection of the dead.

Here we see all overweening pride laid low. Humanity, there is nothing left for you to boast of, for your boasting and hope lie in putting to death all that is your own and seeking the future life that is in Christ. Since we have its first fruits we are already in its midst, living entirely in the grace and gift of God.

"It is God who is active within us, giving us both the will and the achievement, in accordance with his good purpose." Through his Spirit, God also reveals his wisdom in the plan he has preordained for our glory.

God gives power and strength in our labors. "I have toiled harder than all others," Paul says, "but it is not I but the grace of God, which is with me."

God rescues us from dangers beyond all human expectations. "We felt within ourselves that we had received the sentence of death, so that we might not trust in ourselves but in God, who raises the dead; from so great a danger did he deliver us, and does deliver us; we hope in him, for he will deliver us again."

CHAPTER 6

SAINT GREGORY NAZIANZEN

As we saw in the previous chapter, Saint Gregory of Nazianzus (also called Gregory Nazianzen) was a close friend of Saint Basil the Great from the time they were classmates at a university in Athens, Greece. They, along with Saints Athanasius and John Chrysostom, were recognized as the four great Doctors of the Church from the East from the eighth to the sixteenth century, when additional Doctors were named. Gregory Nazianzen was called "the Theologian" because of his scholarly writings about Christian doctrine, and the Christian Demosthenes because of his superb eloquence.

He was born near Nazianzus in Cappadocia, a province in Asia Minor (modern Turkey) in 330. Both of his parents, Gregory Nazianzus the Elder and Nonna, are revered as saints. His father was the bishop of Nazianzus.

After his education in Athens Gregory returned to Nazianzus. When Basil asked him to join him in the monastery he founded in 359, Gregory was glad to accept. He wasn't there long, though, before his father prevailed on him to return home and help him with his diocese and his estate. He was ordained a priest against his will in 362 and continued to work for his father. He managed to prevent a schism when his father made compromises with Arianism, successfully bringing his father back to orthodoxy.

After Basil was named archbishop of Caesarea in 370 he appointed Gregory one of his suffragan bishops and, in 372, named him bishop of Sasima. Sasima was a miserable and unhealthy town and Gregory refused to go there, remaining instead as an auxiliary bishop to his father. This, as one might imagine, caused a temporary cooling off of the friendship between Basil and Gregory, and Basil reproached Gregory for not taking possession of his see.

After his father's death in 374, Gregory retired to a monastery in Seleucia (near modern Baghdad, Iraq), where he spent the next five years in prayer and study. He was still there when Basil died on January 1, 379. He would have been content to stay there, but in 379 he was called to help the Church in Constantinople. The Church in Constantinople had been under Arian dominance, especially during the reign of Emperor Valens. But Valens was now dead and Arianism was no longer imperially protected.

Biographers all note that Gregory was, by nature, shy and retiring. Upon moving to Constantinople, he first stayed at a friend's home. But he recognized his obligation to preach Christian orthodoxy and, mainly because of his eloquent preaching on the Trinity, he quickly became the principal opponent of Arianism. His work culminated in convincing Emperor Theodosius to convene the second ecumenical council, the First Council of Constantinople, in 381.

The council opened with Bishop Meletius presiding, but he died during the council and Gregory was chosen to succeed him. As patriarch of Constantinople, Gregory presided over the council. The council ratified the work of the Council of Nicaea and made appropriate modifications to the Nicene Creed. Besides again condemning Arianism, it also condemned another heresy, Macedonianism, which taught that there exists in the Trinity a hierarchy (instead of an equality) of Persons. Finally, the council declared that the See of Constantinople was second only to the See of Rome in honor and dignity, and the patriarch of Constantinople second only to the pope.

Gregory, though, rather than rejoicing in such an honor, became appalled at the schemes and intrigues of those around him. He resigned from his office and in 382 retired to private life at Nazianzus. He spent the last days of his life in quiet prayer, meditation, and penance. He died on January 25, 389 at age 59.

Gregory Nazianzen is ranked along with Basil

the Great and Gregory of Nyssa as one of the "three Cappadocian Fathers." Besides his sermons, his writings include *Five Theological Orations*, the *Philocalia* (excerpts from Origen), a compilation of Origen's writings which he did with Basil, and a poem titled *De Vita Sua*.

The Church celebrates his feast along with that of Saint Basil on January 2.

From a Sermon by Saint Gregory Nazianzen

Basil and I were both in Athens. We had come, like streams of a river, from the same source in our native land, had separated from each other in pursuit of learning, and were now united again as if by plan, for God so arranged it.

I was not alone at that time in my regard for my friend, the great Basil. I knew his irreproachable conduct, and the maturity and wisdom of his conversation. I sought to persuade others, to whom he was less well known, to have the same regard for him. Many fell immediately under his spell, for they had already heard of him by reputation and hearsay.

What was the outcome? Almost alone of those who had come to Athens to study he was exempted from the customary ceremonies of initiation for he was held in higher honor than his status as a first-year student seemed to warrant.

Such was the prelude to our friendship, the

kindling of that flame that was to bind us together. In this way we began to feel affection for each other. When, in the course of time, we acknowledged our friendship and recognized that our ambition was a life of true wisdom, we became everything to each other: we shared the same lodging, the same table, the same desires, the same goal. Our love for each other grew daily warmer and deeper.

The same hope inspired us: the pursuit of learning. This is an ambition especially subject to envy. Yet between us there was no envy. On the contrary, we made capital out of our rivalry. Our rivalry consisted, not in seeking the first place for oneself but in yielding it to the other, for we each looked on the other's success as his own.

We seemed to be two bodies with a single spirit. Though we cannot believe those who claim that "everything is contained in everything," yet you must believe that in our case each of us was in the other and with the other.

Our single object and ambition was virtue, and a life of hope in the blessings that are to come; we wanted to withdraw from this world before we departed from it. With this end in view we ordered our lives and all our actions. We followed the guidance of God's law and spurred each other on to virtue. If it is not too boastful to say, we found in each other a standard and rule for discerning right from wrong.

Different men have different names, which they owe to their parents or to themselves, that is, to their own pursuits and achievements. But our great pursuit, the great name we wanted, was to be Christians, to be called Christians.

From a Sermon on the Incarnation, by Saint Gregory Nazianzen

The very Son of God, older than the ages, the invisible, the incomprehensible, the incorporeal, the beginning of beginning, the light of light, the fountain of life and immortality, the image of the archetype, the immovable seal, the perfect likeness, the definition and word of the Father: he it is who comes to his own image and takes our nature for the good of our nature, and unites himself to an intelligent soul for the good of my soul, to purify like by like. He takes to himself all that is human, except for sin. He was conceived by the Virgin Mary, who had been first prepared in soul and body by the Spirit; his coming to birth had to be treated with honor, virginity had to receive new honor. He comes forth as God, in the human nature he has taken, one being, made of two contrary elements, flesh and spirit. Spirit gave divinity, flesh received it.

He who makes rich is made poor; he takes on the poverty of my flesh, that I may gain the riches of his divinity. He who is full is made empty; he is emptied for a brief space of his glory, that I may share in his fullness. What is this wealth of goodness? What is this mystery that surrounds me? I received the likeness of God, but failed to keep it. He takes on my flesh, to bring salvation to the image, immortality to the flesh. He enters into a second union with us, a union far more wonderful than the first.

Holiness had to be brought to man by the humanity assumed by one who was God, so that God might overcome the tyrant by force and so deliver us and lead us back to himself through the mediation of his Son. The Son arranged this for the honor of the Father, to whom the Son is clearly obedient in all things.

The Good Shepherd, who lays down his life for the sheep, came in search of the straying sheep to the mountains and hills on which you used to offer sacrifice. When he found it, he took it on the shoulders that bore the wood of the cross, and led it back to the life of heaven.

Christ, the light of all lights, follows John, the lamp that goes before him. The Word of God follows the voice in the wilderness; the bridegroom follows the bridegroom's friend, who prepared a worthy people for the Lord by cleansing them by water in preparation for the Spirit.

We need God to take our flesh and die, that we might live. We have died with him, that we may be purified. We have risen again with him, because we have died with him. We have been glorified with him, because we have risen again with him.

From a Sermon on God's Generosity, by Saint Gregory Nazianzen

Recognize to whom you owe the fact that you exist, that you breathe, that you understand, that you are wise, and, above all, that you know God and hope for the kingdom of heaven and the vision of glory, now darkly and as in a mirror but then with greater fullness and purity. You have been made a son of God, coheir with Christ. Where did you get all this, and from whom?

Let me turn to what is of less importance: the visible world around us. What benefactor has enabled you to look out upon the beauty of the sky, the sun in its course, the circle of the moon, the countless number of stars, with the harmony and order that are theirs, like the music of a harp? Who has blessed you with rain, with the art of husbandry, with different kinds of food, with the arts, with houses, with laws, with states, with a life of humanity and culture, with friendship and the easy familiarity of kinship?

Who has given you dominion over animals, those that are tame and those that provide you with food? Who has made you lord and master of everything on earth? In short, who has endowed you with all that makes man superior to all other living creatures?

Is it not God who asks you now in your turn to show yourself generous above all other creatures and for the sake of all other creatures? Because we have received from him so many wonderful gifts, will we not be ashamed to refuse him this one thing only, our generosity? Though he is God and Lord he is not afraid to be known as our Father. Shall we for our part repudiate those who are our kith and kin?

Brethren and friends, let us never allow ourselves to misuse what has been given us by God's gift. If we do, we shall hear Saint Peter say: "Be ashamed of yourselves for holding on to what belongs to someone else. Resolve to imitate God's justice, and no one will be poor." Let us not labor to heap up and hoard riches while others remain in need. If we do, the prophet Amos will speak out against us with sharp and threatening word: "Come now, you that say: When will the new moon be over, so that we may start selling? When will Sabbath be over, so that we may start opening our treasures?"

Let us put into practice the supreme and primary law of God. He sends down rain on just and sinful alike, and causes the sun to rise on all without distinction. To all earth's creatures he has given the broad earth, the springs, the rivers and the forests. He has given the air to the birds, and the waters to those who live in water. He has given abundantly to all the basic needs of life, not as a private possession, not restricted by law, not divided by boundaries, but as common to all, amply and in rich measure. His gifts are not deficient in any way, because he wanted to give equality of blessing to equality of worth, and to show the abundance of his generosity.

From a Homily on Passover, by Saint Gregory Nazianzen

We are soon going to share in the Passover, and although we still do so only in a symbolic way, the symbolism already has more clarity than it possessed in former times because, under the law, the Passover was, if I may dare to say so, only a symbol of a symbol. Before long, however, when the Word drinks the new wine with us in the kingdom of his Father, we shall be keeping the Passover in a yet more perfect way, and with deeper understanding. He will then reveal to us and make clear what he has so far only partially disclosed. For this wine, so familiar to us now, is eternally new.

It is for us to learn what this drinking is, and for him to teach us. He has to communicate this knowledge to his disciples, because teaching is food, even for the teacher.

So let us take our part in the Passover prescribed by the law, not in a literal way, but according to the teaching of the Gospel; not in an imperfect way, but perfectly; not only for a time, but eternally. Let us regard as our home the heavenly Jerusalem, not the earthly one; the city glorified by angels, not the one laid waste by armies. We are not required to sacrifice young bulls or rams, beasts with horns and hoofs that are more dead than alive and devoid of feeling; but instead, let us join the choirs of angels in offering God upon his heavenly altar a sacrifice of praise. We must now pass through the first veil and approach the second, turning our eyes toward the Holy of Holies. I will say more: we must sacrifice ourselves to God, each day and in everything we do, accepting all that happens to us for the sake of the Word, imitating his passion by our sufferings, and honoring his blood by shedding our own. We must be ready to be crucified.

If you are a Simon of Cyrene, take up your cross and follow Christ. If you are crucified beside him like one of the thieves, now, like the good thief, acknowledge your God. For your sake, and because of your sin, Christ himself was regarded as a sinner; for his sake, therefore, you must cease to sin. Worship him who was hung on the cross because of you, even if you are hanging there yourself. Derive some benefit from the very shame; purchase salvation with your death. Enter paradise with Jesus, and discover how far you have fallen. Contemplate the glories there, and leave the other scoffing thief to die outside in his blasphemy.

If you are a Joseph of Arimathea, go to the one who ordered his crucifixion, and ask for Christ's body. Make your own the expiation for the sins of the whole world. If you are a Nicodemus, like the man who worshiped God by night, bring spices and prepare Christ's body for burial. If you are one of the Marys, or Salome, or Joanna, weep in the early morning. Be the first to see the stone rolled back, and even the angels perhaps, and Jesus himself.

CHAPTER 7

SAINT JOHN CHRYSOSTOM

Saint John Chrysostom is the fourth of the four men — along with Saints Athanasius, Basil, and Gregory Nazianzen — who were considered the great Doctors of the Church from the East until more were added in the sixteenth century.

He was not known as John Chrysostom during his lifetime. "Chrysostom" is a title, Greek for "golden-mouth," which was given to John after his death because of his great eloquence as a preacher. However, his fame rests not only on his reputation for being one of the Church's greatest preachers, but also for his holiness and care for the poor that he demonstrated as a priest in Antioch and patriarch of Constantinople.

John was born about the year 347 in Antioch, Syria, the only son of Secundus, a commander of the imperial troops, and Anthusa, who was left a widow when she was only twenty. His mother, though, was left with sufficient means to see that John received the best secular education available, and John studied law and rhetoric in Antioch under Libanius, recognized as the greatest Roman orator of his time. His religious education was not neglected, however, and he took special studies in Scripture under the Antiochean priest Diodorus of Tarsus, the founder of the "Antiochean School" of biblical interpretation. John was baptized at about the age of twenty.

After his mother's death in 374, John joined one of the communities of monks in the mountains to the south of Antioch. He remained there for four years, leading an austere life of fasting, prayer and study. Then he spent another two years living as a hermit in a cave. However, he overdid his austerity, his health broke down, and he was forced to return to the city in 381. He was ordained a deacon by Saint Meletius shortly before Meletius left for Constantinople where he died as the presiding prelate at the First Council of Constantinople. (He was succeeded by Saint Gregory Nazianzus.)

John served as a deacon for five years. One of his responsibilities was to collect and distribute alms for the care of the poor and sick and it was in carrying out these duties that John obtained firsthand knowledge of the conditions in which these people lived. Afterwards he wrote and spoke forcefully against social injustice, the misuse of wealth, and the neglect of the poor.

When John was about forty, he was ordained a priest in 386 by Bishop Flavian, who immediately delegated almost all the preaching in the cathedral to John, as well as the religious instruction of the people. For the next twelve years, preaching was John's principal occupation and his fame as a preacher spread throughout the Roman Empire. More than seven hundred of these sermons have come down to us, and it was mainly because of them that he was declared a Doctor of the Church.

His sermons probably would not be listened to as avidly today as they were when he delivered them. They are a bit too florid for modern tastes, but that was the style in those days. A modern audience would undoubtedly find the sermons much too long, too, since they always ran longer than an hour and sometimes two hours. But still people came from all over to hear John. It wasn't because of his delivery style, either, since he seems to have had a rather weak voice and his short thin body, large bald head, and straggly beard hardly made him impressive looking. What attracted people to the sermons were the content, John's vast knowledge of all the Scriptures, and the forceful words he used to express his ideas.

Most of John's sermons were homilies on the Scriptures, especially on the Gospels and the Acts of the Apostles. He delivered no less than eighty-eight homilies on the Gospel of John and his homilies on the letters of Saint Paul rank among the best commentaries ever written about them. He is called Doctor of the Eucharist for his beautiful witness to the Real Presence of Christ in the Eucharist.

In 397 Archbishop Nectarius of Constantinople died and the new emperor, Arcadius, was looking for his successor. Theoretically the clergy and laity of a diocese selected their bishop in those days, but for the capital of the empire it was the emperor who actually made the decision. Arcadius followed the advice of his prime minister, Eutropius, who recommended John, the famous orator of Antioch, although several others wanted the position and Archbishop Theophilus of Alexandria was promoting his own candidate.

John was not interested in the office and the people of Antioch definitely didn't want to lose him. But one day John was invited by the imperial commissioner at Antioch to visit a shrine outside the city. Once outside Antioch, the coach sped on to Constantinople; John was kidnaped. John accepted his kidnaping as the will of God and accepted his selection as archbishop of Constantinople. Archbishop Theophilus consecrated him.

John found the Church of Constantinople badly in need of reform. He began the reform at the top, cutting down the expenses for the archbishop's office and living as simply as he did when he was a monk or a priest. He sold the rich furnishings in the palace and used the proceeds to build a hospital for the poor. Next he put an end to unnecessary banquets and exhorted his clergy to follow his example of frugality.

He got in trouble, though, when he began

to preach against the extravagances and immodesty of the wealthy women he saw in Constantinople. This got back to the Empress Eudoxia, who felt personally insulted when John interceded on behalf of a certain widow whose country estate was taken by Eudoxia by dishonest means. There's dispute over whether John actually called Eudoxia a Jezebel, in reference to the biblical wife of King Ahab who plotted the killing of Naboth so Ahab could get his vineyard, but Eudoxia thought he did and began to look for a way to get rid of this troublemaker.

In this she had a willing ally in Archbishop Theophilus of Alexandria. The plot they worked out was a bit complicated, but basically Theophilus landed at Constantinople in June of 403 with several of his suffragan bishops from Egypt. He got together thirty-six bishops in a house in Chalcedon, across the Bosporus from Constantinople, and they issued a sentence of deposition against John and sent it to Emperor Arcadius. One of the accusations was treason, apparently for calling the empress a Jezebel. Upon receiving it, Arcadius issued an order for John's banishment.

John was sent to Bithynia, but he wasn't there long. An earthquake shook Constantinople and this terrified the superstitious Eudoxia so much that she asked Arcadius to recall John, sending John a letter in which she implored him to return and claiming her innocence in his banishment. The people of the city went out to welcome John back while Theophilus and his party fled by night. (One of those in his party was Cyril, a nephew of Theophilus, who succeeded him as archbishop of Alexandria and went on to become a Doctor of the Church; see Chapter 11.)

But John wasn't back in his cathedral for long. Two months later Eudoxia had a silver statue of herself erected in the public square on which the cathedral faced. The pagan revelry that accompanied the unveiling of the statue was so loud that John had trouble conducting services in the cathedral, so he complained to the chief of police about it. The chief reported the matter to Eudoxia, who took it as a personal matter and resolved once again to get rid of John. And, once again, she turned to Theophilus, who advised her that she could have John banished on the grounds that he had violated the canon of an earlier synod held at Antioch which declared that a bishop who had been deposed by a synod could not be reinstated except with the approval of a more important synod.

John refused to abandon his flock. But on Holy Saturday of 404 imperial soldiers broke into the cathedral and attacked those being baptized. John was rescued by his people and was safely guarded in his palace until Pentecost. Then, hoping to keep peace, he secretly surrendered himself and was conducted by imperial troops to

Nicaea. When the people learned about it, a riot broke out and, in the midst of a bloody battle, the cathedral was burned to the ground. (Later Emperor Justinian I erected the magnificent Hagia Sophia Cathedral on the spot.)

John was taken to Cucusus, a little place in the Taurus mountains of Armenia, a trip of 70 days in severe heat. He remained there for three years during which he carried on a large correspondence, comforting and guiding his flock. He also wrote a long letter to Pope Innocent I, telling him the full story of his persecution. The pope responded by excommunicating all three patriarchs of the East: Theophilus; the man who succeeded John as archbishop of Constantinople; and the archbishop of Antioch who, after succeeding Flavian, had become an enemy of John.

Arcadius then retaliated by sending an order that John was to be moved still farther away, to Pityus at the eastern end of the Black Sea. But John was in no condition to travel there, especially in the scorching heat of another summer, and he died on the way, at the chapel of Saint Basiliscus in Comana, Cappadocia, on September 14, 407, at age 60.

His feast day is celebrated on September 13 in the West, November 13 in the East.

From a Homily on the Holy Eucharist, by Saint John Chrysostom

"How can this man give us his flesh to eat?"

If you seek to know the "how," why do you not ask this in the matter of the loaves, how he extended five to so great a number? Because they then only thought of being satisfied, not of seeking the miracle. "But," says someone, "their experience then taught them." Then by reason of that experience these words ought to have been readily received. For to this end he wrought beforehand that strange miracle, that taught by it they might no longer disbelieve what should be said by him afterwards.

These men then at that time reaped no fruit from what was said, but we have enjoyed the benefit in the very realities. Wherefore it is necessary to understand the marvel of the Mysteries, what it is, why it is given, and what is the profit of the action. We become one Body, and "members of his flesh and of his bones." Let the initiated follow what I say. In order then that we may become this not by love only, but in very deed, let us be blended into that flesh. This is effected by the food which he has freely given us, desiring to show the love which he has for us.

On this account he has mixed up himself with us; he that kneaded up his body with ours, that we might be a certain One Thing, like a body joined to a head. For this belongs to them who love strongly; this, for instance, Job implied, speaking of his servants, by whom he was beloved so exceedingly, that they desired to cleave unto his flesh. For they said, to show the strong love which they felt, "Who would give us to be satisfied with his flesh?"

Wherefore this also Christ has done, to lead us to a closer friendship, and to show his love for us; he has given to those who desire him not only to see him, but even to touch, and eat him, and fix their teeth in his flesh, and to embrace him, and satisfy all their love. Let us then return from that table like lions breathing fire, having become terrible to the devil; thinking on our Head, and on the love which he has shown for us. Parents often entrust their offspring to others to feed; "but I," says he, "do not so, I feed you with my own flesh, desiring that you all be nobly born, and holding forth to you good hopes for the future. For he who gives out himself to you here, much more will do so hereafter. I have willed to become your brother, for your sake I shared in flesh and blood, and in turn I give out to you the flesh and the blood by which I became your kinsman."

From a Homily on Paul's Letters, by Saint John Chrysostom

Paul, more than anyone else, has shown us what man really is, and in what our nobility consists, and of what virtue this particular animal is capable. Each day he aimed ever higher; each day he rose up with greater ardor and faced with new eagerness the dangers that threatened him. He summed up his attitude in the words: "I forget what is behind me and push on to what lies ahead." When he saw death imminent, he bade others share his joy: "Rejoice and be glad with me!" And when danger, injustice and abuse threatened, he said: "I am content with weakness, mistreatment and persecution." These he called the weapons of righteousness, thus telling us that he derived immense profit from them.

Thus, amid the traps set for him by his enemies, with exultant heart he turned their every attack into a victory for himself; constantly beaten, abused and cursed, he boasted of it as though he were celebrating a triumphal procession and taking trophies home, and offered thanks to God for it all: "Thanks be to God who is always victorious in us!" This is why he was far more eager for the shameful abuse that his zeal in preaching brought upon him than we are for the most pleasing honors, more eager for death than we are for life, for poverty than we are for wealth; he yearned for toil far more than others yearn for rest after toil. The one thing he feared, indeed dreaded, was to offend God; nothing else could sway him. Therefore, the only thing he really wanted was always to please God.

The most important thing of all to him, however, was that he knew himself to be loved by Christ. Enjoying this love, he considered himself happier than anyone else; were he without it, it would be no satisfaction to be the friend of principalities and powers. He preferred to be thus loved and be the least of all, or even to be among the damned, than to be without that love and be among the great and honored. To be separated from that love was, in his eyes, the greatest and most extraordinary of torments; the pain of that loss would alone have been hell, and endless, unbearable torture.

So too, in being loved by Christ he thought of himself as possessing life, the world, the angels, present and future, the kingdom, the promise and countless blessings. Apart from that love nothing saddened or delighted him; for nothing earthly did he regard as bitter or sweet.

Paul set no store by the things that fill our visible world, any more than a man sets value on the withered grass of the field. As for tyrannical rulers or the people enraged against him, he paid them no more heed than gnats. Death itself and pain and whatever torments might come were but child's play to him, provided that thereby he might bear some burden for the sake of Christ.

Though housed in a narrow prison, Paul dwelt in heaven. He accepted beatings and wounds more readily than others reach out for rewards. Sufferings he loved as much as prizes; indeed he regarded them as his prizes, and therefore called them a grace or gift. Reflect on what this means. "To depart and be with Christ" was certainly a reward, while remaining in the flesh meant struggle. Yet such was his longing for Christ that he wanted to defer his reward and remain amid the fight; those were his priorities.

Now, to be separated from the company of Christ meant struggle and pain for Paul; in fact, it was a greater affliction than any struggle or pain would be. On the other hand, to be with Christ was a matchless reward. Yet, for the sake of Christ, Paul chose the separation.

But, you may say: "Because of Christ, Paul found all this pleasant." I cannot deny that, for he derived intense pleasure from what saddens us. I need not think only of perils and hardships. It was true even of the intense sorrow that made him cry out: "Who is weak that I do not share the weakness? Who is scandalized that I am not consumed with indignation?"

I urge you not simply to admire but also to imitate this splendid example of virtue, for, if we do, we can share his crown as well.

From a Homily on the Gospel of John, by Saint John Chrysostom

After Andrew had stayed with Jesus and had learned much from him, he did not keep this treasure to himself, but hastened to share it with his brother. Notice what Andrew said to him: "We have found the Messiah, that is to say, the Christ." Notice how his words reveal what he has learned in so short a time. They show the power of the master who has convinced them of this truth. They reveal the zeal and concern of men preoccupied with this question from the very beginning. Andrew's words reveal a soul waiting with the utmost longing for the coming of the Messiah, looking forward to his appearing from heaven, rejoicing when he does appear, and hastening to announce so great an event to others. To support one another in the things of the spirit is the true sign of good will between brothers, of loving kinship and sincere affection.

Notice, too, how, even from the beginning, Peter is docile and receptive in spirit. He hastens to Jesus without delay. "He brought him to Jesus," says the evangelist. But Peter must not be condemned for his readiness to accept Andrew's word without much weighing of it. It is probable that his brother had given him, and many others, a careful account of the event; the evangelists, in the interest of brevity, regularly summarize a lengthy narrative. Saint John does not say that Peter believed immediately, but that "he brought him to Jesus." Andrew was to hand him over to Jesus, to learn everything for himself. There was also another disciple present, and he hastened with them for the same purpose.

When John the Baptist said: "This is the Lamb," and, "he baptizes in the Spirit," he left the deeper understanding of these things to be received from Christ. All the more so would Andrew act in the same way, since he did not think himself about to give a complete explanation. He brought his brother to the very source of light, and Peter was so joyful and eager that he would not delay even for a moment.

From a Homily on Repentance, by Saint John Chrysostom

Would you like me to list the paths of repentance? They are numerous and quite varied, and all lead to heaven.

A first path of repentance is the condemnation of your own sins: "Be the first to admit your sins and you will be justified." For this reason, too, the prophet wrote: "I said: I will accuse myself of my sins to the Lord, and you forgave the wickedness of my heart." Therefore, you too should condemn your own sins; that will be enough reason for the Lord to forgive you, for a man who condemns his own sins is slower to commit them again. Rouse your conscience to accuse you within your own house, lest it become your accuser before the judgment seat of the Lord.

That, then, is one very good path of repentance. Another and no less valuable one is to put out of our minds the harm done us by our enemies, in order to master our anger, and to forgive your fellow servants' sins against us. Then our own sins against the Lord will be forgiven us. Thus you have another way to atone for sin: "For if you forgive your debtors, your heavenly Father will forgive you."

Do you want to know of a third path? It consists of prayer that is fervent, careful and comes from the heart.

If you want to hear of a fourth, I will mention almsgiving, whose power is great and far-reaching.

If, moreover, a man lives a modest, humble life, that, no less than the other things I have mentioned, takes sin away. Proof of this is the tax-collector who had no good deeds to mention, but offered his humility instead and was relieved of a heavy burden of sins.

Thus I have shown you five paths of repentance: condemnation of your own sins, forgiveness of our neighbor's sins against us, prayer, almsgiving, and humility.

Do not be idle, then, but walk daily in all these paths; they are easy, and you cannot plead your poverty. For, though you live out your life amid great need, you can always set aside your wrath, be humble, pray diligently and condemn your own sins; poverty is no hindrance. Poverty is not an obstacle to our carrying out the Lord's bidding, even when it comes to that path of repentance which involves giving money (almsgiving, I mean). The widow proved that when she put her two mites into the box!

Now that we have learned how to heal those wounds of ours, let us apply the cures. Then, when we have regained genuine health, we can approach the holy table with confidence, go gloriously to meet Christ, the king of glory, and attain the eternal blessings through the grace, mercy and kindness of Jesus Christ, our Lord.

CHAPTER 8

SAINT AMBROSE

Saint Ambrose is the first, chronologically, of the original four Doctors of the Western Church, the others being Saints Jerome, Augustine, and Pope Gregory the Great. He is known for his learning, his courage, his activism, and his influence on civic life as well as that of the Church. He is also known as the man who baptized Saint Augustine.

Ambrose was born about the year 340 in the palace of the ancient German town of Trier, then a part of Gaul. His father, also named Ambrose, was prefect of southern Gaul, a vast territory that included France, Britain, Spain, the Mediterranean islands, and a region of Africa. His father died when Ambrose was only four or five, and his mother took her three children to Rome, where Ambrose was educated in the classical tradition common for the upper classes of Rome. He became a lawyer and began practicing law in the courts of Rome.

He attracted the notice of Anicius Probus, prefect of Italy, who appointed him assessor. Then, in 370, when he was barely thirty, Emperor

Valentinian I made him governor of Liguria and Aemilia, with residence in Milan, then the administrative capital of the Western Empire. He proved to be a popular governor.

In 374, after Ambrose had been governor for four years, Bishop Auxentius of Milan (who happened to be an Arian) died. The city was torn over the election of his successor, some demanding another Arian and others a Catholic. Ambrose went to the church where the people were meeting and gave a talk in which he exhorted them to make their choice peacefully. While he was speaking, a voice called out, "Ambrose, bishop!" Soon the whole assembly took up the cry and Ambrose found himself being elected bishop unanimously. At the time he was still a catechumen, not yet baptized.

Emperor Valentinian had to give his consent to having an imperial officer elected bishop, and a report of the election was sent to him. Ambrose, too, wrote to Valentinian asking that he withhold his consent, but Valentinian replied that it gave him the greatest pleasure that one of his governors was deemed fit for the episcopal office. Ambrose was baptized and then, a week later, consecrated bishop on December 7, 374, when he was about thirty-five years old.

Ambrose was quite conscious of his lack of knowledge about theological matters, so he began to study the Scriptures and the works of Church

Fathers such as Origen and Basil. Meanwhile, he gave up his worldly possessions and began to live a life of simplicity, maintaining a vigorous schedule of prayer, including the daily Eucharist and night vigils. He made it easy for his people to see and speak to him at any time and he became a popular bishop as he had been a popular governor.

He had already been an articulate speaker and now became an eloquent preacher. He has been described in the pulpit as a passionate little man with a high forehead, a long melancholy face and great eyes. His sermons were often modeled on Cicero and sometimes borrowed ideas from pagan Roman authors. One of his pet themes, though, not found in the Roman authors, was praise for the state and virtue of virginity. He had many consecrated virgins under his direction, including his sister Marcellina. It is said that mothers tried to keep their daughters from hearing his sermons.

It was his sermons that first attracted Augustine to him. Augustine's *Confessions* describe some animated discussions between the two Doctors of the Church, and there have always been disputes about just how much influence Ambrose had on Augustine. There is no doubt, however, that Ambrose had a great deal of influence over Augustine's mother, Monica, and that Augustine held him in great esteem.

Ambrose became a champion of orthodox

Christianity against Arianism, writing several treatises against the Arians. He also wrote treatises on the psalms, the sacraments, and Christian ethics, as well as doctrinal works on faith and the Holy Spirit.

He was also a composer of hymns, some of which have come down to us. These were usually sung in what is known today as Ambrosian Chant, a forerunner of Gregorian Chant. It was a simple rhythm with a single note for each syllable of text. It was used in what is still today known as the Ambrosian Rite, one of the few non-Roman rites of the Catholic Church to endure in Western Christianity.

Ambrose was the first of the Doctors of the Church to write in Latin. As the Roman Empire declined in the West he helped keep Latin alive by starting it on its new course in the service of the Catholic Church.

Ambrose was a bishop for only a few months when Emperor Valentinian died. Valentinian's brother, Valens, was then emperor in the East and Valentinian's son, Gratian, became emperor in the West. At that time, the Goths invaded Roman territories in the East and Gratian was determined to go to his uncle's aid. Valens, though, was an ardent protector of the Arians and Gratian asked Ambrose to instruct him about that heresy. So Ambrose wrote a treatise titled *To Gratian, on the Faith*. In 378, Valens was killed in the battle of

Adrianople and an orthodox Spanish general, Theodosius, vanquished the Goths. Gratian recognized Theodosius as emperor of the East.

Gratian was murdered in 383 and the empress Justina, who had been the wife of Valentinian, became regent for her son, Valentinian II, then twelve years old. The usurper Maximus was preparing to attack Italy and Justina asked Ambrose to negotiate with him. Ambrose traveled to Trier, met with Maximus, and persuaded him to confine his conquests to Gaul, Spain, and Britain. Historians consider it the first time a Christian minister was asked to intervene in an important political matter.

Ambrose then won a victory in another affair. Gratian had removed an altar to the pagan Goddess of Victory from the senate-house in Rome. Now a group of pagan senators petitioned Valentinian II to have the altar restored. Ambrose objected. Both the leader of the senators, Quintus Aurelius Symmachus, and Ambrose prepared arguments, which were read before Valentinian. He decided in favor of Ambrose, saying, "My father did not take away the altar, nor was he asked to put it back. I therefore follow him in changing nothing that was done before my time."

Usually, though, Ambrose was on the opposite side of Justina and Valentinian II because they were Arians. At a council in Aquileia in 382, Ambrose had been successful in deposing two Arian bishops in spite of Justina's opposition. In 385, Justina had Valentinian demand the Portian basilica, located just outside Milan, for use of the Arians. Ambrose refused, saying that he could not surrender a temple of God to heretics. Then Valentinian demanded the larger new basilica of the Apostles, located in the city. Again Ambrose refused. At one point, soldiers were ordered to seize the larger basilica and they entered it while Ambrose was preaching in a small chapel. But they laid down their arms and prayed with the Catholics.

In January Justina persuaded Valentinian to issue a law outlawing Catholic assemblies and forbidding anyone, under pain of death, to oppose Arian assemblies. Ambrose simply ignored the law. On Palm Sunday he preached against giving up churches to the Arians and Justina decided to bring the matter to a head. Imperial troops surrounded the church, where the Catholics had barricaded themselves. On Easter Sunday they were still there. To pass the time, Ambrose taught them hymns he had composed, divided them into two choirs, and had them sing alternate stanzas. In one of his sermons that week he proclaimed, "The emperor is in the Church, not over it."

Justina backed down because, once again, she needed Ambrose. It became known that Maximus was again preparing to invade Italy so, once again, Justina asked Ambrose to stop the invasion. And, once again Ambrose traveled to Trier. This time, though, the mission was unsuccessful, Maximus did invade Italy, and Justina and Valentinian fled to Greece to ask the assistance of the Eastern emperor, Theodosius. He declared war on Maximus, defeated and executed him, and returned Justina and Valentinian to their territories. From then on, though, Theodosius was the real ruler of the entire empire.

Soon disagreements arose between Ambrose and Theodosius. The first one reveals the Church's attitude towards Jews in the fourth century. In Mesopotamia, some Christians had destroyed a Jewish synagogue. When Theodosius heard of it, he ordered the bishop there to rebuild it. The bishop appealed to Ambrose who wrote a letter to Theodosius saying that no Christian bishop should have to pay for the erection of a building to be used for false worship. Ambrose preached against Theodosius to his face and there was a discussion between them in the church. Ambrose refused to continue with the Mass until he received a promise of pardon for the bishop. Ambrose won.

In 390 there was a terrible massacre in Thessalonica. In retaliation for a riot by the people in which several people were killed, Theodosius's troops killed seven thousand people. Ambrose wrote a severe letter to Theodosius, telling him that "what was done at Thessalonica is unparalleled in the memory of man," and urging him to penance. Theodosius did the public penance.

Theodosius died in 395 with Ambrose at his side. At his funeral, Ambrose praised Theodosius. Referring to the massacre at Thessalonica, he said, "He, an emperor, was not ashamed to perform the public penance which lesser individuals shrink from, and to the end of his life he never ceased to grieve for his crime."

Ambrose himself died two years later, on Good Friday, April 4, 397, at age fifty-seven, and was buried in Milan. The Church celebrates his feast on December 7.

Morning Hymn, by Saint Ambrose

Eternal Lord, the world who made,
Who rules the day and night's dark shade
And sets the time to hours, that we
May never faint or weary be.

Hark to the herald of the morn
Who vigil through the dark has borne,
To travelers in the dark a light
That separates the night from night.

The daystar hears and at his call
Loosens the sky from night's black thrall,
While roaming brigands at his word
Their mischief leave and sheathe their sword....

So let us rise in eager haste:
The cock forbids us life to waste.
He stirs the sluggards and doth show
Those who refuse the wrong they do....

O Jesus, aid us where we stray,
Look down and set us on our way.
Beneath thy gaze our faltering cease
And in our tears guilt turns to peace.

Shine on our senses with thy light
And from our minds put sleep to flight.
Let us our first songs raise to thee
And all our hymns be praise to thee.

Evening Hymn, by Saint Ambrose

God that all things didst create
And the heavens doth regulate,
Who doth clothe the day with light,
And with gracious sleep the night....

Day sinks; we thank thee for thy gift.
Night comes; to thee again we lift
Our prayers and vows and hymns, that we
Against all ills defended be....

That so, when shadows round us creep
And all is hid in darkness deep,
Faith may not feel the gloom; and night
Borrow from faith's clear gleam new light....

From snares of sense, Lord, keep us free
And let our hearts dream but of thee.
Let not the envious foe draw near
To vex our quiet rest with fear.

Hail we the Father and the Son
And Son's and Father's Spirit, one
Blest Trinity whom all obey;
Guard thou the souls that to thee pray.

From the Book *On Virginity,* by Saint Ambrose

You are one of God's people, of God's family, a virgin among virgins; you light up your grace of body with your splendor of soul. More than others you can be compared to the Church. When you are in your room, then, at night, think always on Christ, and wait for his coming at every moment.

This is the person Christ has loved in loving you, the person he has chosen in choosing you. He enters by the open door; he has promised to come in, and he cannot deceive. Embrace him, the one you have sought; turn to him, and be enlightened; hold him fast, ask him not to go in haste, beg him not to leave you. The Word of God moves swiftly; he is not won by the lukewarm, nor held fast by the negligent. Let your soul be attentive to his word; follow carefully the path God tells you to take, for he is swift in his passing.

What does his bride say? "I sought him, and did not find him; I called him, and he did not hear me." Do not imagine that you are displeasing to him although you have called him, asked him, opened the door to him, and that this is the reason why he has gone so quickly; no, for he allows us to be constantly tested. When the crowds pressed him to stay, what does he say in the Gospel? "I must preach the word of God to other cities, because I have been sent for that." But even if it seems to you that he has left you, go out and seek him once more.

Who but holy Church is to teach you how to hold Christ fast? Indeed, she has already taught you, if you only understood her words in Scripture: "How short a time it was when I left them before I found him whom my soul has loved. I held him fast, and I will not let him go."

How do we hold him fast? Not by restraining chains or knotted ropes but by bonds of love, by spiritual reins, by the longing of the soul.

If you also, like the bride, wish to hold him fast, seek him and be fearless of suffering. It is often easier to find him in the midst of bodily torments, in the very hands of persecutors.

His bride says: "How short a time it was after I left them." In a little space, after a brief moment, when you have escaped from the hands of your persecutors without yielding to the powers of this world, Christ will come to you, and he will not allow you to be tested for long.

Whoever seeks Christ in this way, and finds him, can say: "I held him fast, and I will not let him go before I bring him into my mother's house, into the room of her who conceived me." What is this "house," this "room," but the deep and secret places of your heart?

Maintain this house, sweep out its secret recesses until it becomes immaculate and rises as a spiritual temple for a holy priesthood, firmly secured by Christ, the cornerstone, so that the Holy Spirit may dwell in it.

Whoever seeks Christ in this way, whoever prays to Christ in this way, is not abandoned by him; on the contrary, Christ comes again and again to visit such a person, for he is with us until the end of the world.

From *The Explanations of the Psalms*, by Saint Ambrose

What is more pleasing than a psalm? David expresses it well: "Praise the Lord, for a song of praise is good; let there be praise of our God with gladness and grace." Yes, a psalm is a blessing on the lips of the people, a hymn in praise of God, the assembly's homage, a general acclamation, a word that speaks for all, the voice of the Church, a confession of faith in song. It is the voice of complete assent, the joy of freedom, a cry of happiness, the echo of gladness. It soothes the temper, distracts from care, lightens the burden of sorrow. It is a source of security at night, a lesson in wisdom by day. It is a shield when we are afraid, a celebration of holiness, a vision of serenity, a promise of peace and harmony. It is like a lyre, evoking harmony from a blend of notes. Day begins to the music of a psalm. Day closes to the echo of a psalm.

In a psalm, instruction vies with beauty. We sing for pleasure. We learn for our profit. What experience is not covered by a reading of the psalms? I come across the words: "A song for the beloved," and I am aflame with desire for God's love. I go through God's revelation in all its beauty, the intimations of resurrection, the gifts of his promise. I learn to avoid sin. I see my mistake in feeling ashamed of repentance for my sins.

What is a psalm but a musical instrument to give expression to all the virtues? The psalmist of old used it, with the aid of the Holy Spirit, to make earth reecho the music of heaven. He used the dead gut of strings to create harmony from a variety of notes, in order to send up to heaven the song of God's praise. In doing so he taught us that we must first die to sin, and then create in our lives on earth a harmony through virtuous deeds, if the grace of our devotion is to reach up to the Lord.

David thus taught us that we must sing an interior song of praise, like Saint Paul, who tells us: "I shall pray in spirit, and also with understanding; I shall sing in spirit, and also with understanding." We must fashion our lives and shape our actions in the light of the things that are above. We must not allow pleasure to awaken bodily passions, which weigh our soul down instead of freeing it. The holy prophet told us that his songs of praise were to celebrate the freeing of his soul, when he said: "I shall sing to you, God, on the lyre, holy one of Israel; my lips will rejoice when I have sung to you, and my soul also, which you have set free."

From the Beginning of the Treatise *On the Mysteries*, by Saint Ambrose

We gave a daily instruction on right conduct when the readings were taken from the history of the patriarchs or the maxims of Proverbs. These readings were intended to instruct and train you, so that you might grow accustomed to the ways of our forefathers, entering into their paths and walking in their footsteps, in obedience to God's commands.

Now the season reminds us that we must speak of the mysteries, setting forth the meaning of the sacraments. If we had thought fit to teach these things to those not yet initiated through baptism, we should be considered traitors rather than teachers. Then, too, the light of the mysteries is of itself more effective where people do not know what to expect than where some instruction has been given beforehand.

Open then your ears. Enjoy the fragrance of eternal life, breathed on you by means of the sacraments. We explained this to you as we celebrated the mystery of "the opening" when we said: "Effetha, that is, be opened." Everyone who was to come for the grace of baptism had to understand what he was to be asked, and must remember what he was to answer. This mystery was celebrated by Christ when he healed the man who was deaf and dumb, in the Gospel which we proclaimed to you.

After this, the holy of holies was opened up for you; you entered into the sacred place of regeneration. Recall what you were asked; remember what you answered. You renounced the devil and his works, the world and its dissipation and sensuality. Your words are recorded, not on a monument to the dead but in the book of the living.

There you saw the Levite, you saw the priest, you saw the high priest. Do not consider their outward form but the grace given by their ministries. You spoke in the presence of angels, as it is written: "The lips of a priest guard knowledge, and men seek the law from his mouth, for he is the angel of the Lord almighty." There is no room for deception, no room for denial. He is an angel whose message is the kingdom of Christ and eternal life. You must judge him, not by his appearance but by his office. Remember what he handed on to you, weigh up his value, and so acknowledge his standing.

You entered to confront your enemy, for you intended to renounce him to his face. You turned toward the east, for one who renounced the devil turns toward Christ and fixes his gaze directly on him.

Chapter 9

SAINT JEROME

Almost every biography of Saint Jerome begins by saying that he was the most learned biblical scholar of the Fathers of the Church. He was the translator of the Vulgate, the Latin version of the Scriptures that the Council of Trent declared to be the authentic text used by the Church. He is one of the four original Doctors of the Church because of his contributions to Christian thought, particularly in the area of biblical scholarship.

But Jerome was also undoubtedly the most contentious and outspoken of the Doctors of the Church, a fearless critic of other Christians with whom he disagreed — including, for a time, Saint Augustine. He was quick to get angry and just as quick to feel remorse afterward. Some paintings of Jerome show him striking his breast with a stone, which prompted one pope to remark, "You do well to carry that stone, for without it the Church would never have canonized you."

Eusebius Hieronymus Sophronius (Jerome's full name) was born about the year 342 at Stridon, a small town in Dalmatia near Aquileia. His na-

tive language was Illyrian. He was sent to Rome
for his education and there became fluent in both
Latin and Greek, reading the literatures of both lan-
guages with great pleasure. While in Rome, he later
wrote, he lost some of the Christian piety that had
been imbued in him at home, but he also stated
that he enjoyed visiting the tombs of martyrs in
the catacombs, deciphering the inscriptions on the
walls. He was baptized when he was eighteen by
Pope Liberius.

Jerome's intellectual curiosity then led him
to leave Rome in order to explore other parts of
the world. Accompanied by his boyhood friend
Bonosus, he first went to Aquileia, where he came
to know Rufinus, a monk and theologian who was
later to become a bitter opponent. He then moved
on to Trier, in Gaul. Here he had a religious awak-
ening that led him to renounce all secular pursuits
and to dedicate himself to God. Always a scholar,
he copied some of Saint Hilary's books and started
to build up a library.

He returned to Aquileia, where the bishop,
Saint Valerian, had attracted so many good men
that the clergy there became famous throughout
the Western Church. After a few years, though,
some kind of conflict developed and Jerome
headed east with several friends. After visiting Athens, Bithynia, Galatia, Pontus, Cappadocia, and
Cilicia, they arrived in Antioch, Syria about the year
374.

In Antioch, two of his traveling companions died, and Jerome became ill. (A third companion returned to Italy.) Later, in a letter to Saint Eustochium, Jerome wrote that, during delirium caused by a high fever, he thought that he was standing before the judgment seat of Christ. Christ asked him who he was and he replied that he was a Christian. "Thou liest," Christ replied. "Thou art a Ciceronian, not a Christian: for where thy treasure is, there is thy heart also." It was a condemnation of Jerome's preference for Roman literature instead of Christian writings.

Jerome then withdrew into the wilderness of Chalcis, about fifty miles from Antioch, where he lived as a hermit for four years, spending the time in study and austerity. Among the things he studied was Hebrew, and he also wrote a biography of Saint Paul of Thebes. During those four years, he had many attacks of illness and also suffered from temptations against purity. He described his temptations and his battle against them in a letter to Saint Eustochium quoted later in this chapter.

The Church at Antioch was then racked with doctrinal and disciplinary disputes, and divided into three parts. The monks of the desert of Chalcis took sides and wanted Jerome to do so, too. Jerome wrote for guidance to Pope Damasus, but received no answer. He wrote again and this time probably received a reply, although the answer is not extant. Whatever Pope Damasus may have replied, Jerome ended up acknowledging Paulinus, the leader of one of the parties, as bishop of Antioch. When he left the desert, Jerome was ordained a priest by Paulinus, but he consented to be ordained only on the condition that he would not have to serve in any church. Indeed, it is believed that he never celebrated the Eucharist.

After his ordination in 380, he moved to Constantinople, where he studied the Scriptures under Saint Gregory Nazianzen. When Gregory resigned as bishop of Constantinople in 382, Jerome went to Rome with Bishop Paulinus of Antioch to attend a council which Pope Damasus had convened to deal with the schism in Antioch. Jerome was appointed secretary of that council and so impressed the pope that he kept him in Rome as his own personal secretary.

While he was serving as secretary to Pope Damasus, Jerome was asked by the pope to prepare a revised text, based on the original Greek, of the Latin New Testament. He also revised the Latin psalter. In his spare time, he fostered a new movement of asceticism among some of Rome's noble ladies, several of whom were later canonized. Chief among them were Paula and her daughters Blesilla and Eustochium, to whom he later was to address many of his famous letters.

Pope Damasus died after Jerome was in Rome for only two years. During that time he had earned a reputation for learning and holiness, but his outspokenness also created enemies. He wrote diatribes against worldly women (quoted later in this chapter) and certain members of the Roman clergy. About the latter, he wrote: "All their anxiety is about their clothes.... You would take them for bridegrooms rather than for clerics; all they think about is knowing the names and houses and doings of rich ladies." In retaliation, he was attacked for his simplicity and even for his walk and smile, and scandalous gossip soon circulated about his relations with Paula.

After Pope Damasus died in 384 and Pope Siricius was elected, Jerome decided it was better for him to return to the East. He went first to Cyprus and then to Antioch. Here he was joined by Paula, Eustochium, and other Roman women who had resolved to spend their lives with Jerome in the Holy Land. They moved to Bethlehem where Paula financed the building of a monastery for men near the Basilica of the Nativity, and houses for three communities of women. Paula became head of one of them and, after her death, Eustochium succeeded her. Jerome chose to live in a cave beside the cave where Jesus was born. Jerome's cave continues to be visited by pilgrims to Bethlehem yet today. He opened both a school and a hospice for pilgrims in Bethlehem.

Jerome spent the rest of his life in Bethlehem. Here, from 390 to 410, he finished translating the Bible into Latin, work which he had begun in Rome. After translating the New Testament from the Greek, he translated the Old Testament directly from the Hebrew. When he learned that the Book of Tobias and part of Daniel had been composed in Chaldaic, he learned that language, too. The only books he did not translate were the Books of Wisdom, Ecclesiasticus, Baruch, and the two Books of the Maccabees.

But he did more than translate the Bible. He wrote commentaries on the Old and New Testaments; continued the *Ecclesiastical History* begun by Eusebius of Caesarea, bringing it up to 378; published *De Viris Illustribus*, presenting the leading ecclesiastical writers of the time; translated some of Origen's work; and wrote a large number of letters (published in three volumes) and a variety of controversial treatises. Those treatises were mainly on heresies that kept popping up — mainly Arianism, Origenism, and Pelagianism. Jerome could not keep silent about controversial religious issues.

One of the controversies concerned the perpetual virginity of Mary. While in Rome, Jerome had written a book that disputed the claim of Helvidius that Mary had not remained a virgin but had had other children by Saint Joseph after Christ's birth. That idea was put forward again by Jovinian, and Paula's son-in-law, Pammachius, sent some of Jovinian's writings to Jerome. Jerome wrote two books against Jovinian. He was so vehement in his expressions in support of virginity that he seemed to deprecate marriage. He went so far as to call marriage evil, saying that even a later martyrdom could barely wash its taint from a woman. When Pammachius took offense at this, Jerome composed an *Apology to Pammachius* in which he quoted from some of his earlier work to show that he regarded marriage as a good and honorable state.

Another controversy, with a Gallic priest named Vigilantius (Jerome sarcastically called him Dormantius — sleepy — the opposite of vigilant), concerned priestly celibacy and the veneration of saints' relics. Jerome defended celibacy, writing that monks should fly from temptations and dangers when they distrusted their own strength to resist those temptations. As for the veneration of relics, he wrote that no Christian had ever adored the martyrs as gods or worshiped their relics, but honored them in order that the respect paid to them might be reflected back to God.

His opponent in the dispute over Origenism was his former friend Rufinus, who had moved to Jerusalem. Jerome himself was a great admirer of Origen but felt that some errors had crept into his writings. Rufinus enthusiastically upheld Origen's authority. The animosity that resulted in the dispute between Jerome and Rufinus greatly distressed Saint Augustine.

Then Augustine learned how easy it was to

offend Jerome because he, too, unwillingly became involved in a controversy with him. The controversy began with a disagreement about the second chapter of Saint Paul's Letter to the Galatians and Augustine's first letters on the topic unintentionally provoked Jerome. Augustine had to use considerable tact to soothe Jerome's feelings. When a letter from Jerome failed to reach Augustine, Jerome felt insulted that Augustine didn't reply and wrote angrily to tell him so. Augustine replied softly, and humbly, "I entreat you again and again to correct me firmly when you see me standing in need of it; for though the office of bishop [which Augustine held] is greater than that of priest, yet in many respects Augustine is inferior to Jerome."

Jerome's days of work and prayer in his cave in Bethlehem were interrupted several years before the end of his life when Pelagianists, protected by Bishop John of Jerusalem, sent a troop of thugs to Bethlehem to disperse the monks and nuns living there under Jerome's direction. Some monks were beaten, a deacon was killed, monasteries were set on fire, and Jerome had to go into hiding.

Jerome was severely ill the last two years of his life. Then, his sight and voice almost gone and his body emaciated, he died peacefully on September 30, 420. He was buried under the Church of the Nativity at Bethlehem, but in the thirteenth century his body was moved to Rome where it now lies somewhere in the Basilica of Saint Mary Major.

The Church celebrates his feast on September 30.

From a Letter to Saint Eustochium, by Saint Jerome

In the remotest part of a wild and stony desert, burnt up with the heat of the scorching sun so that it frightens even the monks that inhabit it, I seemed to myself to be in the midst of the delights and crowds of Rome. In this exile and prison to which for the fear of hell I had voluntarily condemned myself, I many times imagined myself witnessing the dancing of the Roman maidens as if I had been in the midst of them. In my cold body and in my parched-up flesh, which seemed dead before its death, passion was still able to live. Alone with this enemy, I threw myself in spirit at the feet of Jesus, watering them with my tears, and I tamed my flesh by fasting whole weeks. I am not ashamed to disclose my temptations, but I grieve that I am not now what I then was.

From Another Letter to Saint Eustochium, by Saint Jerome

[Beware of worldly women who] paint their cheeks with rouge and their eyelids with antimony, whose plastered faces, too white for human beings, look like idols; and if in a moment of forgetfulness they shed a tear it makes a furrow where it rolls down the painted cheek; women to whom years do not bring the gravity of age, who load their heads with other people's hair, enamel a lost youth upon the wrinkles of age, and affect a maidenly timidity in the midst of a troop of grandchildren.

* * *

Today you see many women packing their wardrobes with dresses, changing their tunics every day, and even so unable to keep ahead of the moth. The more scrupulous wear one dress until it is threadbare, but yet have their boxes full of clothes. Their parchments are dyed purple, gold is melted for the lettering, their books are decorated with jewels, and Christ lies naked and dying at their door. When they stretch out their hands to give anything, they blow a trumpet.

Only lately I saw the greatest lady in Rome — I will not tell her name, for this is not a satire — in the church of the Blessed Peter with her eunuchs in front of her, dispensing money to the poor with her own hands so as to be thought the more pious. To each one she gave a penny, and then, as you might easily know by experience would happen, an old woman full of years and rags, ran forward suddenly to get a second penny, but when her turn came, she got not a penny but a blow from the lady's fist and for her terrible crime paid with her blood!

From the Prologue of a Commentary on Isaiah, by Saint Jerome

I interpret as I should, following the command of Christ: "Search the Scriptures," and, "Seek and you shall find." Christ will not say to me what he said to the Jews: "You erred, not knowing the Scriptures and not knowing the power of God." For if, as Paul says, Christ is the power of God and the wisdom of God, and if the man who does not know Scripture does not know the power and wisdom of God, then ignorance of Scripture is ignorance of Christ.

Therefore, I will imitate the head of a household who brings out of his storehouse things both new and old, and says to his spouse in the Song of Songs: "I have kept for you things new and old, my beloved." In this way permit me to explain Isaiah, showing that he was not only a prophet, but an evangelist and an apostle as well. For he says about himself and the other evangelists: "How beautiful are the feet of those who preach good news, of those who announce peace." And God speaks to him as if he were an apostle: "Whom shall I send, who will go to my people?" And he answers: "Here I am; send me."

No one should think that I mean to explain the entire subject matter of this great book of Scripture in one brief sermon, since it contains all the mysteries of the Lord. It prophesies that Emmanuel is to be born of a virgin and accomplish marvelous works and signs. It predicts his death, burial and resurrection from the dead as the Savior of all men. I need say nothing about the natural sciences, ethics and logic. Whatever is proper to holy Scripture, whatever can be expressed in human language and understood by the human mind, is contained in the book of Isaiah. Of these mysteries the author himself testifies when he writes: "You shall be given a vision of all things, like words in a sealed scroll. When they give the writings to a wise man, they will say: Read this. And he will reply: I cannot, for it is sealed. And when the scroll is given to an uneducated man and he is told: Read this, he will reply: I do not know how to read."

Should this argument appear weak to anyone, let him listen to the Apostle: "Let two or three prophets speak, and let others interpret; if, however, a revelation should come to one of those who are seated there, let the first one be quiet." How can they be silent, since it depends on the Spirit who speaks through his prophets whether they remain silent or speak? If they understood what they were saying, all things would be full of wisdom and knowledge. But it was not the air vibrating with the human voice that reached their ears, but rather it was God speaking within the soul of the prophets, just as another prophet says: "It is an angel who spoke to me"; and again, "Crying out in our hearts, Abba, Father," and, "I shall listen to what the Lord God says within me."

From a Sermon on Psalm 42, by Saint Jerome

"As the deer longs for running water, so my soul longs for you, my God." Just as the deer longs for running water, so do our newly baptized members, our young deer, so to speak, also yearn for God. By leaving Egypt and the world, they have put Pharaoh and his entire army to death in the waters of baptism. After slaying the devil, their hearts long for the springs of running water in the Church. These springs are the Father, the Son and the Holy Spirit. Jeremiah testifies that the Father is like a fountain when he says: "They have forsaken me, the fountain of living water, to dig for themselves cisterns, broken cisterns that can hold no water." In another passage we read about the Son: "They have forsaken the fountain of wisdom." And again, John says of the Holy Spirit: "Whoever drinks the water I will give him, that water shall become in him a fountain of water, springing up into eternal life." The evangelist explains that the Savior said this of the Holy Spirit. The testimony of these texts establishes beyond doubt that the three fountains of the Church constitute the mystery of the Trinity.

These are the waters that the heart of the believer longs for, these are the waters that the heart of the newly baptized yearns for when he says: "My heart thirsts for God, the living fountain." This is not a weak, faint desire to see God; rather the newly baptized actually burn with desire and thirst for God. Before they received baptism, they used to ask one another: "When shall I go and see the face of God?" Now their quest has been answered. They have come forward and they stand in the presence of God. They have come before the altar and have looked upon the mystery of the Savior.

Having received the body of Christ, and being reborn in the life-giving waters, they speak up boldly and say: "I shall go into God's marvelous dwelling place, his house." The house of God is the Church, his marvelous dwelling place, filled with joyful voices giving thanks and praise, filled with all the sounds of festive celebration.

This is the way you should speak, you newly baptized, for you have now put on Christ. Under our guidance, by the word of God you have been lifted out of the dangerous waters of this world like so many little fish. In us the nature of things has been changed. Fish taken out of the sea die; but the apostles have fished for us and have taken us out of the sea of this world so we could be brought from death to life. As long as we were in the world, our eyes looked down into the abyss and we lived in filth. After we were rescued from the waves, we began to look upon the sun and look up at the true light. Confused in the presence of so much joy, we say: "Hope in God, for I shall again praise him, in the presence of my Savior and my God."

CHAPTER 10

SAINT AUGUSTINE

By common assent, Saint Augustine is considered to be the greatest of the Fathers and Doctors of the Church, surpassed by no one in the whole history of Christian theology. His enormous contributions to Christian theology have been preeminent for the past sixteen hundred years. He enjoyed a virtual monopoly on theological thought in the Catholic Church until the time of Saint Thomas Aquinas in the thirteenth century. Still today Saint Augustine is quoted in the *Catechism of the Catholic Church* far more often than any other ecclesiastical writer. (Augustine is quoted eighty-five times while Thomas Aquinas is quoted fifty-eight times.) Also, excerpts from Augustine's writings appear in the Office of Readings — part of the Liturgy of the Hours — far more often than any other ecclesiastical writer. (There are eighty-two excerpts from Augustine's writings. Saints Ambrose and Leo the Great are tied for second with twenty-six, and there are only five from Thomas Aquinas.)

The Church has a lot of Augustine's writing

from which to choose since he wrote one hundred thirteen books, two hundred eighteen letters, and more than five hundred sermons. His subject matter included everything from the psychological complexity of his *Confessions* to political insights in the *City of God* (his two most famous books), to commentaries on the feasts of saints, to treatises against the heresies of his day.

Most of what we know about Augustine's early life comes to us directly from his spiritual autobiography. Augustine called it *Confessiones* in Latin, and it is usually translated as *Confessions* in English. However, the historian Garry Wills believes that this word "misses the complexity of a word in which Augustine intuited an entire theology." Therefore, throughout Wills' book *Saint Augustine*, he calls Augustine's book *The Testimony* instead of *Confessions*. The book, sometimes called history's first great autobiography, gives us an account of Augustine's life, including his sins and failings, but it is more concerned with the operation of God's grace in his life.

Augustine was born on November 13, 354 in Tagaste, Numidia, North Africa. His father, Patricius, was a pagan (until his conversion a year before his death) and his mother, Monica, was a devout Christian. It was apparent at an early age that Augustine had a brilliant mind and, when he was sixteen, he was sent to the major African city of Carthage (in modern Tunisia) to study law. In-

‹ stead, he turned to literary affairs. He also suc-
cumbed to the temptations of youth and took a
mistress. Having done so, though, he was faithful
to her for fifteen years, until he sent her away while
he was in Milan. With his mistress, he fathered a
child whom he named Adeodatus (given by God)
when he was seventeen. Meanwhile, his father
died.

While in Carthage, Augustine read the
Hortensius of Cicero and became interested in
philosophy. The philosophy he became attracted
to, though, was Manichaeism, which taught that
there are two eternal first principles: God, the cause
of all good, and matter, the cause of all evil. He
was to remain a Manichaean for nine years before
becoming disillusioned with the philosophy, especially after a noted Manichaean teacher named
Faustus was unable to answer his questions satis-
factorily.

He conducted schools of rhetoric and grammar at both Tagaste and Carthage for nine years.
Meanwhile, his mother continued her prayers that
he would become a Christian. She not only prayed,
but tried to stay close to him, sometimes closer than
Augustine wanted. One night in 383, when he was
twenty-nine, Augustine told Monica that he was
going to the dock to say good-bye to a friend.
Instead, he, his mistress, and their child took a ship
to Rome. There he opened a school to teach rhetoric, as he had done in Africa. He soon learned,

though, that parents in Rome were accustomed to switching their children from school to school in order to avoid paying fees.

When he learned that there was a position open for a teacher of rhetoric in the imperial capital of Milan, he applied for the position, and got it. There he made the acquaintance of Ambrose, Milan's bishop, and began to listen to his eloquent sermons. At the same time, he immersed himself in Neoplatonism, the philosophy based on the teachings of Plato developed by Plotinus in the third century. It stressed the mystical and anti-materialistic, advocating the idea of the transcendent One, or Unity, from whom all things in the universe proceeded through a series of emanations.

Meanwhile, Monica, after learning that Augustine had sailed for Rome, made arrangements to follow him there. By the time she arrived, though, Augustine had left for Milan, so she went on to Milan. There she took Ambrose as her spiritual adviser as she continued to pray for Augustine's conversion. She wanted to see him married to a woman of his own station in life and convinced him to send his mistress back to Africa, where it is believed she entered a convent.

Augustine, Monica, Adeodatus, Augustine's brother Navigius (who had accompanied Monica) and several of Augustine's friends moved into a villa where Augustine continued to study. He also prayed for chastity, but halfheartedly; his prayer was, "Lord, give me chastity, but not yet." He wrote in *Confessions* that he was "afraid that Thou might hear me too soon, and heal me of the disease which I wished to have satisfied rather than cured."

One day an African Christian named Pontitian visited Augustine and his friend Alipius. He talked about the book *Life of Saint Anthony*, written by Athanasius, and was surprised to learn that Augustine wasn't familiar with either the book or Saint Anthony. After Pontitian left, Augustine and Alipius went out into the garden and Augustine suffered from the throes of his conflict. The story of what happened next is quoted from *Confessions* later in this chapter.

Leaving the garden, Augustine told his mother that he was ready to become a Christian. This happened in September of 386. Augustine then quit his position as a teacher of rhetoric and moved with his mother, son, and friends into a country house at Cassiciacum, near Milan. He spent the winter in retreat, studying, praying, and conversing with the others about his new-found faith. He returned to Milan and was baptized by Ambrose on Holy Saturday in 387 along with Alipius and Augustine's son Adeodatus, who was then fifteen years old.

That fall, Augustine decided to return to Tagaste. He and his party traveled to Ostia, Rome's seaport, to await a ship to North Africa. While they were there, Monica died in November 387. Some of the most moving passages in *Confessions* describe Monica's last days and her death. After her death, Augustine went back to Rome and spoke out publicly against Manichaeism. It was ten months before he and his party sailed back to Africa, where they settled in Augustine's home in Tagaste.

There they set up a kind of monastic community, holding everything in common and devoting themselves to prayer, fasting, and good works. Augustine wrote and began to instruct others with his discourses and books. Soon he had a reputation for both holiness and brilliance. He continued to live at Tagaste for three years. During that time, his beloved son Adeodatus died when he was seventeen.

Augustine had no intention of becoming a priest or bishop. He was well aware that there might be an attempt to make him a bishop, as happened to Ambrose, so he purposely stayed away from cities where the see was vacant. However, in 391 he happened to be in the city of Hippo, where the bishop there, Valerius, had spoken to the people about his need for a priest to assist him. When Augustine came into the church, the congregation swept him forward to Valerius and clamored for his ordination. Augustine acquiesced. He then moved to Hippo and established a community in a house adjoining the church similar to the one he had had in Tagaste. In 395 he was consecrated coadjutor bishop and, when Valerius died soon afterward, succeeded him as bishop of Hippo. He was forty-one.

Augustine was bishop of Hippo for almost thirty-five years. During all that time he continued his writing and preaching. He also established a monastic community for all the priests, deacons, and sub-deacons who lived with him in the episcopal residence. They renounced all private property and lived simple and frugal lives. The furnishings in the home were plain, they used no silverware except spoons, and they ate from earthenware or wooden plates.

Augustine also founded a community of religious women, with his sister Perpetua as its abbess. A letter he wrote to her, together with two sermons on the subject, comprised the Rule of Saint Augustine. Although originally written for women and largely forgotten after Augustine's death, the Rule was revived in the eleventh century and became the basis for the constitutions of the Augustinian Canons, the Augustinian Friars, the Dominicans, the Ursulines, and other religious orders. In broad terms, the Rule called for poverty, obedience, celibacy, and a strict monastic life.

During his years as bishop, Augustine found himself constantly defending the Church against the heresies of his day, notably Manichaeism, Donatism, and Pelagianism. Manichaeism, named for a third-century Persian named Mani (or

Manichaeus in Latin), was the religious and ethi-cal doctrine that Augustine originally embraced as a youth. It taught that there are two equal, eternal principles: one of good, light and spirit; the other of darkness, matter, and evil.

Donatism was named after Donatus, a priest who became a schismatic bishop of Carthage in 312. The Donatists challenged the legitimacy of Caecilian as bishop of Carthage because he had been consecrated by Felix of Aptunga, who had lapsed during the persecution of Diocletian and thus, they believed, could no long validly admin-ister the sacraments. The Donatist schism split the African hierarchy into two almost equal parts. In combating this heresy and schism, Augustine taught that the efficacy of the sacraments depends not on the worthiness of their ministers but on the power of Christ, who is their true minister. He presented the Catholic ideal of unity centered in the See of Peter and did it so compellingly that the Donatist heresy died.

Pelagius was named after an Irish monk who lived from 355 to 425, roughly the same years as Augustine. Pelagius rejected the doctrine of origi-nal sin, denied the necessity of grace for salvation, and taught that humans can achieve salvation by their own efforts alone. This contrasted sharply with Augustine's beliefs and teachings. Augustine has been called the Doctor of Grace because he defended the Church's doctrine that grace is necessary for salvation.

The extensive body of theology propounded by Augustine came to be known as Augustinianism. Based especially on such doctrines as grace, original sin, and the Fall, it remained unchallenged as the orthodox teaching of the Church until the time of Saint Thomas Aquinas — eight centuries. Augustine's philosophy was based on that of Plato, just as Thomas Aquinas's was based on that of Aristotle. In effect, Augustine Christianized Platonism while Thomas Aquinas Christianized Aristotelianism.

Despite his prolific literary productivity, Augustine wrote carefully, sometimes spending many years on his more important works. He wrote *Confessions* from 397 to 400. He wrote his most theologically deep treatise, *On the Trinity*, over a period of sixteen years from 400 to 416. He began *On Christian Doctrine* in 397 and didn't finish it until 426.

In 410, the Goths plundered Rome. One of the results of that disaster was an outbreak of hostility toward Christians by pagans who claimed that the city's destruction came because the ancient pagan gods had been forsaken. Partially in answer to these accusations, Augustine in 413 began to write his greatest book, *The City of God*, although he didn't finish it until 426. It contrasted the City of God, a heavenly society, with the secular City of the World. It said that all the virtues of past history — of the Romans, the Greeks, the Hebrews — find fulfillment in Christ, and only Christianity embraces both a history back to the beginning of time and a future until the end of time.

In 426 Augustine named Heraclius as his auxiliary and tried to go into semi-retirement so he could concentrate on his writings. He finished both *The City of God* and *On Christian Doctrine.* Then he reviewed the great body of his past writings and produced *Retractions*, candidly and severely correcting mistakes he thought he had made.

In 428 the Vandals invaded Africa and spread desolation and destruction in their path. They reached Hippo in May of 430 and began a siege that was to last for fourteen months. Augustine, though, did not live through it. He became ill during the summer of 430, although he retained his senses and intellectual faculties to the end. He died peacefully on August 28, 430, a few months short of his eighty-sixth birthday.

The Church celebrates his feast on August 28, the day after the feast of Saint Monica.

Excerpts from *Confessions,* by Saint Augustine

Too late have I love you, O Beauty of ancient days, yet ever new! Too late I loved you! And behold, you were within, and I abroad, and there I searched for you; I was deformed, plunging amid those fair forms, which you had made. You were with me, but I was not with you. Things held me far from you — things which, if they were not in you, were not at all. You called, and shouted, and burst my deafness. You breathed odors and I drew in breath — and I pant for you. I tasted, and I hunger and thirst. You touched me, and I burned for your peace.

* * *

A little garden there was to our lodging, which we had the use of, as of the whole house; for the master of the house, our host, was not living there. There had the tumult of my breast hurried me, where no man might hinder the hot contention wherein I had engaged with myself, until it should end as You know, I knew not. I retired then into the garden, and Alipius, on my steps. For his presence did not lessen my privacy; or how could he forsake me so disturbed? We sat down as far removed as might be from the house....

But when a deep consideration had from the secret bottom of my soul drawn together and heaped up all my misery in the sight of my heart, there arose a mighty storm, bringing a mighty shower of tears. Which that I might pour forth wholly, in its natural expressions, I rose from Alipius: solitude was suggested to me as fitter for the business of weeping; so I retired so far that even his presence could not be a burden to me....

I cast myself down I know not how, under a certain fig tree, giving full vent to my tears; and the floods of my eyes gushed out an acceptable sacrifice to Thee. And, not indeed in these words, yet to this purpose, I spoke much unto Thee: "And thou, O Lord, how long? How long, Lord, will You be angry, for ever? Remember not our former iniquities." For I felt that I was held by them. I sent up these sorrowful words: How long, how long, "tomorrow, and tomorrow?" Why not now?

So was I speaking and weeping in the most bitter contrition of my heart, when lo! I head from a neighboring house a voice, as of boy or girl, I know not, chanting, and often repeating: "Take up and read; take up and read." Instantly, my countenance altered, I began to think most intently whether children were wont in any kind of play to sing such words: nor could I remember ever to have heard the like.

So checking the torrent of my tears, I arose; interpreting it to be no other than a command from God to open the book, and read the first chapter I should find. For I had heard of Anthony, that coming in during the reading of the Gospel, he received the admonition, as if what was being read was spoken to him: "Go, sell all that thou hast, and give to the poor, and thou shalt have treasure in heaven, and come and follow me": and by such oracle he was forthwith converted unto Thee.

Eagerly then I returned to the place where Alipius was sitting; for there had I laid the volume of the Apostle when I arose. I seized, opened, and in silence read that section on which my eyes first fell: "Not in rioting and drunkenness, not in chambering and wantonness, not in strife and envying; but put on the Lord Jesus Christ and make no provision for the flesh, in concupiscence." No further would I read; nor needed I: for instantly at the end of this sentence, by a light as it were of serenity infused into my heart, all the darkness of doubt vanished away.

* * *

The day now approaching whereon [my mother Monica] was to depart this life ... it came to pass ... that she and I stood alone, leaning in a certain window, which looked into the garden of the house where we now lay, at Ostia; where removed from the din of men, we were recuperating from the fatigues of a long journey, for the voyage. We were discoursing then together, alone, very sweetly....

As we spoke, my mother said to me, "Son, for my own part I have no further delight in anything in this life. What I do here any longer, and to what end I am here, I know not, now that my hopes in this world are accomplished. One thing there was for which I desired to linger for a while in this life, that I might see you a Catholic Christian before I died. My God has done this for me more abundantly, that I should now see you withal, despising earthly happiness, become His servant: what do I here?"

What answer I made her, I remember not. For scarce five days after, or not much more, she fell sick of a fever; and in that sickness one day she fell into a swoon, and was for a while withdrawn from these visible things. We hastened round her; but she was soon brought back to her senses; and looking on me and my brother standing by her, said to us inquiringly, "Where was I?" And then looking fixedly on us, with grief amazed: "Here," she said, "shall you bury your mother."…

On the ninth day of her sickness, and the fifty-sixth of her age, and the thirty-third of mine, was that religious and holy soul freed from the body. I closed her eyes; and there flowed a mighty sorrow into my heart, which was overflowing into tears; my eyes at the same time, by the violent command of my mind, drank up their fountain wholly dry; and woe was me in such a strife! But when she breathed her last, the boy Adeodatus burst out into a loud lament; then, checked by us all, held his peace. In like manner also a childish feeling in me, which was, through my heart's youthful voice, finding its vent in weeping, was checked and silenced. For we thought it not fitting to solemnize that funeral with tearful lament, and groanings; for thereby do they for the most part express grief for the departed, as though unhappy, or altogether dead; whereas she was neither unhappy in her death, nor altogether dead.…

May she rest in peace with the husband before and after whom she had never any; whom she obeyed, "with patience bringing forth fruit" unto Thee, that she might win him also unto Thee. And inspire, O Lord my God, inspire Thy servants my brethren, Thy sons my masters, whom with voice and heart, and pen I serve, that so many as shall read these Confessions, may at Thy altar remember Monica Thy handmaid, with Patricius, her husband, by whose bodies Thou brought me into this life, how, I know not.

Excerpts from *The City of God*, by Saint Augustine

We said in our earlier books that it was God's pleasure to propagate all mankind from one man, both to keep in human nature a likeness to one society and also to make its original unity a means of concord in heart. Nor would any of mankind have died had not the first two — one of whom was made from the other and the other of nothing — incurred this punishment by their disobedience. For they committed so great a sin that their whole nature was thereby depraved and the same degree of corruption and necessity of death was transmitted to all their offspring. And thereupon death's power by this just punishment became so great over man that all would have been cast headlong into the second death which has no end had not the merciful grace of God acquitted some from it. And hence it comes to pass that although mankind is divided into many nations, distinct in language, training, habit, and fashion, yet there are but two sorts of men, who do properly make the two cities of which we speak. The one is a city of men who live according to the flesh, and the other a city of men who live according to the Spirit, each after his kind. And when they attain their desire, both live in their peculiar peace.

* * *

Now God, foreknowing all things, could not but know that man would fall; therefore we must found our city on his prescience and ordinance, not on what we know not and he has not revealed. For man's sin could not disturb God's decree nor force him to change his resolve. God foreknew and anticipated both how bad the man he had made would become and what good he meant to produce from his badness. For though God is said to change his intention, as the Scriptures figuratively say he repented, etc., yet this is from the point of view of man's hope or Nature's order, not of his own prescience. So then God made man upright and consequently good in his will; otherwise he could not have been upright. This good will was God's work, man being thus created. The evil will which was in man before his evil deed was rather a falling away from the work of God to its own work than any work in itself.

* * *

Now God had made man in his own image, placed him in Paradise above all creatures, given him all things in abundance and laid no hard or lengthy commands on him but merely that one brief requirement of obedience to show that he himself was Lord of that creature from whom should come a free service. But when he was thus disregarded, there followed his righteous sentence, which was that man, who might have kept his commandment and been spiritual in body became thenceforth carnal in mind, and because he had before delighted in his pride, now tasted of God's justice, becoming not, as he had desired, fully his own master but falling even below himself and becoming the slave of him who had taught him sin, exchanging his sweet liberty for a wretched bondage. By his own will he was dead in spirit, though unwilling to die in the flesh. He had lost eternal life and was condemned to eternal death, did not God's good grace deliver him.

From a Christmas Sermon by Saint Augustine

Our Lord Jesus Christ, the eternal creator of all things, today became our Savior by being born of a mother. Of his own will he was born for us today, in time, so that he could lead us to his Father's eternity. God became man so that man might become God. The Lord of the angels became man today so that man could eat the bread of angels.

Today, the prophecy is fulfilled that said: "Pour down, heavens, from above, and let the clouds rain the just one: let the earth be opened and bring forth a savior." The Lord who had created all things is himself now created, so that he who was lost would be found. Thus man, in the words of the psalmist, confesses: "Before I was humbled, I sinned." Man sinned and became guilty; God is born a man to free man from his guilt. Man fell, but God descended; man fell miserably, but God descended mercifully; man fell through pride, God descended with his grace.

My brethren, what miracles! What prodigies! The laws of nature are changed in the case of man. God is born. A virgin becomes pregnant with man. The Word of God marries the woman who knows no man. She is now at the same time both mother and virgin. She becomes a mother, yet she remains a virgin. The virgin bears a son, yet she does not know man; she remains untouched, yet she is not barren. He alone was born without sin, for she bore him without the embrace of a man, not by the concupiscence of the flesh but by the obedience of the mind.

Sermon on Christ's Passion,
by Saint Augustine

The passion of our Lord and Savior Jesus Christ is the hope of glory and a lesson in patience.

What may not the hearts of believers promise themselves as the gift of God's grace, when for their sake God's only Son, co-eternal with the Father, was not content only to be born as man from human stock but even died at the hands of the men he had created?

It is a great thing that we are promised by the Lord; but far greater is what has already been done for us, and which we now commemorate. Where were the sinners, what were they, when Christ died for them? When Christ has already given us the gift of his death, who is to doubt that he will give the saints the gift of his own life? Why does our human frailty hesitate to believe that mankind will one day live with God?

Who is Christ if not the Word of God? "In the beginning was the Word, and the Word was with God, and the Word was God." This Word of God "was made flesh and dwelt among us." He had no power of himself to die for us: he had to take from us our mortal flesh. This was the way in which, though immortal, he was able to die; the way in which he chose to give life to mortal men: he would first share with us, and then enable us to share with him. Of ourselves we had no power to live, nor did he of himself have the power to die.

Accordingly, he effected a wonderful exchange with us, through mutual sharing: we gave him the power to die, he will give us the power to live.

The death of the Lord our God should not be a cause of shame for us; rather, it should be our greatest hope, our greatest glory. In taking upon himself the death that he found in us, he has most faithfully promised to give us life in him, such as we cannot have of ourselves.

He loved us so much that, sinless himself, he suffered for us sinners the punishment we deserved for our sins. How then can he fail to give us the reward we deserve for our righteousness, for he is the source of righteousness? How can he, whose promises are true, fail to reward the saints when he bore the punishment of sinners, though without sin himself?

Brethren, let us then fearlessly acknowledge, and even openly proclaim, that Christ was crucified for us; let us confess it, not in fear but in joy, not in shame but in glory.

CHAPTER 11

SAINT CYRIL OF ALEXANDRIA

Saint Cyril of Alexandria is known best for championing the doctrine that Mary is the Mother of God because he presided over the Council of Ephesus that proclaimed Mary to be *Theotokos* (Greek for God-bearer). Because of his writings defending the dogma that Jesus had two natures in one person, he has been called the Doctor of the Incarnation, just as Saint Augustine was called the Doctor of Grace. However, as we will see, not all of what Cyril did can be applauded by modern Catholics.

Cyril was born in Alexandria, Egypt in 376. He was the nephew of the patriarch of Alexandria, Theophilus. This is the archbishop who connived with Empress Eudoxia to depose and exile Saint John Chrysostom (see Chapter 8). In 403 Cyril accompanied Theophilus to Constantinople where Theophilus presided at the synod across the Bosporus that deposed John.

Theophilus died in 412 and Cyril succeeded him as archbishop and patriarch of Alexandria. He began his episcopacy by ruthlessly exerting his authority. First he closed and pillaged the churches

of the Novatians, named for an antipope who
taught that Christians who had lapsed from their
faith during persecutions could not return to the
fold.

Next he requested and received permission
from Emperor Theodosius to drive the Jews out
of Alexandria. This incurred the wrath of the governor, Orestes, and also led to the brutal death of
Hypatia, a pagan woman of noble birth who was
famous as a teacher of Platonism. Hypatia was a
consulter to Governor Orestes, and word got back
to the Catholics in Alexandria that Hypatia had
turned Orestes against Cyril. In 417 a mob attacked
Hypatia in the streets, pulling her out of her chariot.
Some reports state that the mob tore her body to
pieces while other accounts say that she was flayed
alive with a whip made from abalone shells. There
seems to be no evidence, though, that Cyril himself had any personal role in this murder, or that
he approved it.

Cyril's principal battle was against Nestorianism. It was named after Nestorius, a priest of
Antioch who was named archbishop of Constantinople in 428. He denied that Mary could be the
mother of God, insisting that she could be the
mother only of Jesus' humanity. The effect of this
was to deny the unity of the divine and human
natures in Jesus. Nestorius objected to the term
Theotokos for Mary, saying that there were two distinct persons in Christ, the divine and the human,

and that Mary was the mother only of the human person, not of the divine person. Cyril saw that this clearly was not what the Nicene Creed says. Orthodox doctrine taught that Christ's two natures were combining in one person. He wrote Nestorius a letter pointing that out and Nestorius responded with haughtiness and contempt.

Both Cyril and Nestorius appealed to Pope Celestine I, who in 430 called a council in Rome to examine the matter. Convinced that Nestorius was teaching heresy, the pope excommunicated him and sent a letter deposing him unless he retracted his errors. He also appointed Cyril to see that the sentence was carried out. Cyril tried to do so, sending Nestorius twelve propositions to be signed by him as proof of his orthodoxy. Nestorius, though, remained as stubborn as ever.

In those days the pope's authority was not yet widely recognized; it was still the Roman emperor who wielded authority. So Emperor Theodosius II convened the third ecumenical council, the Council of Ephesus, in modern Turkey, in 431. The pope was invited, but he did not attend. Instead he appointed Cyril as his representative.

When Cyril arrived in Ephesus, he took charge immediately. He convened the council even though many of those invited, especially the bishops of the Church at Antioch, had not yet arrived. Nestorius was in Ephesus but refused to attend the council. About two hundred bishops were present and they quickly found Nestorius guilty of "distinct blasphemy against the Son of God." They proclaimed Mary truly the God-bearer, the mother of the one person who was truly God and truly man. The council also condemned Pelagianism, which held that humans can attain salvation through the efforts of their natural powers and free will.

Nestorius, naturally, refused to accept the council's decision. He gathered together bishops who agreed with him and held his own council.

Then things got a bit crazy at the Council of Ephesus. Archbishop John and forty-one other Antiochene bishops finally arrived and became angry with Cyril for convening the council in their absence and for the way he ramrodded Nestorius's condemnation through. John managed to take control of the council, deposed Cyril and accused him of heresy. Both sides then appealed to Emperor Theodosius, who had both Cyril and Nestorius arrested and kept in confinement. They were imprisoned for three months, until three legates arrived from Pope Celestine. They examined all that had been done and approved Cyril's conduct. Cyril then was released and he returned to Alexandria.

Archbishops Cyril of Alexandria and John of Antioch continued to have their differences after the council, each condemning the other. But they reconciled in 433 after John proposed a theological formula which he hoped would satisfy everybody. It stated that the "union of two natures had been achieved and because of this union we confess that the holy virgin is *Theotokos*, because the Word of God had been made flesh and been made man." Cyril accepted this formula and it was then approved by the pope, who by that time was Sixtus III.

Cyril continued as archbishop of Alexandria until his death in 444 at age sixty-eight. Besides his writings on the Incarnation, he is known for his commentaries on the Trinity, the Gospels of John and Luke and other Scriptures, and his letters and sermons. His refutation of the work *Against the Galileans* by Julian the Apostate, who had been emperor from 361 to 363, is considered the last of the great apologies for the faith during the Roman era.

Cyril was proclaimed a Doctor of the Church by Pope Leo XIII in 1882. His feast is celebrated in the West on June 27, in the East on June 9.

From a Homily at the Council of Ephesus, by Saint Cyril of Alexandria

I see here a joyful company of Christian men met together in ready response to the call of Mary, the holy and ever-virgin Mother of God. The great grief that weighed upon me is changed into joy by your presence, venerable Fathers. Now the beautiful saying of David the psalmist — "How good and pleasant it is for brothers to live together in unity" — has come true for us.

Therefore, holy and incomprehensible Trinity, we salute you at whose summons we have come together to this church of Mary, the Mother of God.

Mary, Mother of God, we salute you. Precious vessel, worthy of the whole world's reverence, you are an ever-shining light, the crown of virginity, the symbol of orthodoxy, an indestructible temple, the place that held him whom no place can contain, mother and virgin. Because of you the holy gospels could say: "Blessed is he who comes in the name of the Lord."

We salute you, for in your holy womb was confined him who is beyond all limitation. Because of you the holy Trinity is glorified and adored; the cross is called precious and is venerated throughout the world; the heavens exult; the angels and archangels make merry; demons are put to flight; the devil, that tempter, is thrust down from heaven; the fallen race of man is taken up on high; all creatures possessed by the madness of idolatry have attained knowledge of the truth; believers receive holy baptism; the oil of gladness is poured out; the Church is established throughout the world; pagans are brought to repentance.

What more is there to say? Because of you the light of the only-begotten Son of God has shone upon those who sat in darkness and in the shadow of death; prophets pronounced the word of God; the apostles preached salvation to the Gentiles; the dead are raised to life, and kings rule by the power of the holy Trinity.

Who can put Mary's high honor into words? She is both mother and virgin. I am overwhelmed by the wonder of this miracle. Of course no one could be prevented from living in the house he had built for himself, yet who would invite mockery by asking his own servant to become his mother?

Behold then the joy of the whole universe. Let the union of God and man in the Son of the Virgin Mary fill us with awe and adoration. Let us fear and worship the undivided Trinity as we sing the praise of the ever-virgin Mary, the holy temple of God, and of God himself, her Son and spotless Bridegroom. To him be glory for ever and ever. Amen.

From a Letter by Saint Cyril of Alexandria

That anyone could doubt the right of the holy Virgin to be called the Mother of God fills me with astonishment. Surely she must be the Mother of God if our Lord Jesus Christ is God, and she gave birth to him! Our Lord's disciples may not have used those exact words, but they delivered to us the belief those words enshrine, and this has also been taught us by the holy fathers.

In the third book of his work on the holy and consubstantial Trinity, our father Athanasius, of glorious memory, several times refers to the holy Virgin as "Mother of God." I cannot resist quoting his own words: "As I have often told you, the distinctive mark of holy Scripture is that it was written to make a twofold declaration concerning our Savior; namely, that he is and has always been God, since he is the Word, Radiance and Wisdom of the Father; and that for our sake in these latter days he took flesh from the Virgin Mary, Mother of God, and became man."

Again further on he says: "There have been many holy men, free from all sin. Jeremiah was sanctified in his mother's womb, and John while still in the womb leaped for joy at the voice of Mary, the Mother of God." Athanasius is a man we can trust, one who deserves our complete confidence, for he taught nothing contrary to the sacred books.

The divinely inspired Scriptures affirm that the Word of God was made flesh, that is to say, he was united to a human body endowed with a rational soul. He undertook to help the descendants of Abraham, fashioning a body for himself from a woman and sharing our flesh and blood, to enable us to see in him not only God, but also, by reason of this union, a man like ourselves.

It is held, therefore, that there are in Emmanuel two entities, divinity and humanity. Yet our Lord Jesus Christ is nonetheless one, the one true Son, both God and man; not a deified man on the same footing as those who share the divine nature by grace, but true God who for our sake appeared in human form. We are assured of this by Saint Paul's declaration: "When the fullness of time came, God sent his Son, born of a woman, born under the law, to redeem those who were under the law and to enable us to be adopted as sons."

From a Commentary on the Gospel of John, by Saint Cyril of Alexandria

The Lord calls himself the vine and those united to him branches in order to teach us how much we shall benefit from our union with him, and how important it is for us to remain in his love. By receiving the Holy Spirit, who is the bond of union between us and Christ our Savior, those who are joined to him, as branches are to a vine, share in his own nature.

On the part of those who come to the vine, their union with him depends upon a deliberate act of the will; on his part, the union is effected by grace. Because we had good will, we made the act of faith that brought us to Christ, and received from him the dignity of adoptive sonship that made us his own kinsmen, according to the words of Saint Paul: "He who is joined to the Lord is one spirit with him."

The prophet Isaiah called Christ the foundation, because it is upon him that we as living and spiritual stones are built into a holy priesthood to be a dwelling place for God in the spirit. Upon no other foundation than Christ can this temple be built. Here Christ is teaching the same truth by calling himself the vine, since the vine is the parent of its branches, and provides their nourishment.

From Christ and in Christ, we have been reborn through the Spirit in order to bear the fruit of life; not the fruit of our old, sinful life but the fruit of a new life founded upon our faith in him and our love for him. Like branches growing from a vine, we now draw our life from Christ, and we cling to his holy commandment in order to preserve this life. Eager to safeguard the blessing of our noble birth, we are careful not to grieve the Holy Spirit who dwells in us, and who makes us aware of God's presence in us.

Let the wisdom of John teach us how we live in Christ and Christ lives in us: "The proof that we are living in him and he is living in us is that he has given us a share in his Spirit." Just as the trunk of the vine gives its own natural properties to each of its branches, so, by bestowing on them the Holy

Spirit, the Word of God, the only-begotten Son of the Father, gives Christians a certain kinship with himself and with God the Father because they have been united to him by faith and determination to do his will in all things. He helps them to grow in love and reverence for God, and teaches them to discern right from wrong and to act with integrity.

From a Commentary on Saint Paul's Letter to the Romans, by Saint Cyril of Alexandria

Though many, we are one body, and members one of another, united by Christ in the bonds of love. "Christ has made Jews and Gentiles one by breaking down the barrier that divided us and abolishing the law with its precepts and decrees." This is why we should all be of one mind and if one member suffers some misfortune, all should suffer with him; if one member is honored, all should be glad.

Paul says: "Accept one another as Christ accepted you, for the glory of God." Now accepting one another means being willing to share one another's thoughts and feelings, bearing one another's burdens, and "preserving the unity of the Spirit in the bond of peace." This is how God accepted us in Christ, for John's testimony is true and he said that God the Father "loved the world so much that he gave his own Son for us." God's Son was given as a ransom for the lives of us all. He has delivered us from death, redeemed us from death and from sin.

Paul throws light on the purpose of God's plan when he says that Christ became the servant of the circumcised to show God's fidelity. God had promised the Jewish patriarchs that he would bless their offspring and make them as numerous as the stars of heaven. This is why the divine Word himself, who as God holds all creation in being and is the source of its well-being, appeared in the flesh and became man. He came into this world in human flesh not to be served, but, as he himself said, to serve and to give his life as a ransom for many.

Christ declared that his coming in visible form was to fulfill the promise made to Israel. "I was sent only to the lost sheep of the house of Israel," he said. Paul was perfectly correct, then, in saying that Christ became a servant of the circumcised in order to fulfill the promise made to the patriarchs and that God the Father had charged him with this task, as also with the task of bringing salvation to the Gentiles, so that they too might praise their Savior and Redeemer as the Creator of the universe. In this way God's mercy has been extended to all men, including the Gentiles, and it can be seen that the mystery of the divine wisdom contained in Christ has not failed in its benevolent purpose. In the place of those who fell away the whole world has been saved.

SAINT PETER CHRYSOLOGUS

In Chapter 8 we saw that Saint John of Antioch and Constantinople was given the title "Chrysostom," Greek for "golden-mouth," because of his preaching ability. It's a similar case with this Doctor of the Church. Peter of Ravenna was given the title "Chrysologus," Greek for "golden-worded," for exactly the same reason. In fact, Christians of the West gave Peter this title precisely to make him equivalent to John Chrysostom, the preacher in the East. It was a time when there was already considerable competition between the Church of the East and the Church of the West.

Peter's biography is short because he did not move around from one position to another, and he did not have a particularly exciting life. He was born in Imola, a town in eastern Emilia, Italy, in 406. He received his education there and was ordained a deacon by Cornelius, the local bishop. When he was only twenty-seven he was appointed archbishop of Ravenna by Pope Sixtus III and he continued in that position until his death in 450 at age forty-four. Before his death he returned to his birthplace, Imola.

In the fifth century, Ravenna, a city on the Adriatic Sea in eastern Italy, had assumed a more important role in both civil and ecclesiastical history, mainly because of Barbarian invasions of most of the rest of Italy. The western court was moved to Ravenna from Rome by Emperor Honorius at the beginning of the century, before Alaric and his Visigoths sacked Rome in 410. When Honorius moved to Ravenna, Pope Innocent I converted it into a metropolitan see. Then, in 418, after the death of Pope Zosimus, two men — Boniface and Eulalius — were elected and consecrated pope by different constituencies, and Emperor Honorius called a synod of bishops in Ravenna to try to solve the problem. The synod was unsuccessful at unraveling the situation, but subsequent events made Boniface the true pope and Eulalius an antipope.

Those events, though, happened before Peter was consecrated as archbishop of Ravenna. When Peter became archbishop, Emperor Valentinian III, a ten-year-old boy, and his mother, Galla Placidia, resided in the city. Peter enjoyed good relations with them. In fact, the emperor's mother was so inspired by Peter's sermons that she became one of his most ardent patrons.

Peter is known almost entirely for his powerful sermons, and it was for them that he was named a Doctor of the Church by Pope Benedict

XIII in 1729. The sermons were collected by Bishop Felix of Ravenna in the eighth century, and one hundred seventy-six of them have come down to us. They cover biblical texts, the Apostles' Creed, the Blessed Virgin, and other subjects. They are all very short because he wanted to retain the attention of his listeners, and they are full of moral applications. They are historically significant because they show how Christians lived in fifth-century Ravenna. They cannot, though, indicate the fervor with which Peter preached. He is said to have preached with such vehemence that he sometimes became speechless from excitement.

Peter is also known for his loyalty to the pope. A few years before his death, Eutyches, a monk in Constantinople and the leader of the heresy known as Monophysitism, wrote to Church leaders, including Peter, seeking support for his belief that Christ's divine nature absorbed his human nature, that his human body was different from normal human bodies. Peter replied: "In the interest of peace and the faith, we cannot judge in matters of faith without the consent of the Roman bishop." Monophysitism was condemned by the Council of Chalcedon in 451, a year after Peter's death, as we will see in the next chapter on Saint Leo the Great.

The Church celebrates the feast of Saint Peter Chrysologus on July 30.

From a Sermon on the Incarnation,
by Saint Peter Chrysologus

A virgin conceived, bore a son, and yet remained a virgin. This is no common occurrence, but a sign; no reason here, but God's power, for he is the cause, and not nature. It is a special event, not shared by others; it is divine, not human. Christ's birth was not necessity, but an expression of omnipotence, a sacrament of piety for the redemption of men. He who made man without generation from pure clay made man again and was born from a pure body. The hand that assumed clay to make our flesh deigned to assume a body for our salvation. That the Creator is in his creature and God is in the flesh brings dignity to man without dishonor to him who made him.

Why then, man, are you so worthless in your own eyes and yet so precious to God? Why render yourself such dishonor when you are honored by him? Why do you ask how you were created and so not seek to know why you were made? Was not this entire visible universe made for your dwelling? It was for you that the light dispelled the overshadowing gloom; for your sake was the night regulated and the day measured, and for you were the heavens embellished with the varying brilliance of the sun, the moon and the stars. The earth was adorned with flowers, groves and fruit; and the constant marvelous variety of lovely living things was created in the air, the fields, and the seas for you, lest sad solitude destroy the joy of God's new creation. And the Creator still works to devise things that can add to your glory. He has made you in his image that you might in your person make the invisible Creator present on earth; he has made you his legate, so that the vast empire of the world might have the Lord's representative. Then in his mercy God assumed what he made in you; he wanted now to be truly manifest in man, just as he had wished to be revealed in man as in an image. Now he would be in reality what he had submitted to be in symbol.

And so Christ is born that by his birth he might restore our nature. He became a child, was fed, and grew that he might inaugurate the one perfect age to remain forever as he had created it. He supports man that man might no longer fall. And the creature he had formed of earth he now makes heavenly; and what he had endowed with a human soul he now vivifies to become a heavenly spirit. In this way he fully raised man to God, and left in him neither sin, nor death, nor travail, nor pain, nor anything earthly, with the grace of our Lord Christ Jesus, who lives and reigns with the Father in the unity of the Holy Spirit, now and forever, for all the ages of eternity. Amen.

From a Lenten Sermon
by Saint Peter Chrysologus

There are three things, my brethren, by which faith stands firm, devotion remains constant, and virtue endures. They are prayer, fasting and mercy. Prayer knocks at the door, fasting obtains, mercy receives. Prayer, mercy and fasting: these three are one, and they give life to each other.

Fasting is the soul of prayer, mercy is the life-blood of fasting. Let no one try to separate them; they cannot be separated. If you have only one of them or not all together, you have nothing. So if you pray, fast; if you fast, show mercy; if you want your petition to be heard, hear the petition of others. If you do not close your ear to others you open God's ear to yourself.

When you fast, see the fasting of others. If you want God to know that you are hungry, know that another is hungry. If you hope for mercy, show mercy. If you look for kindness, show kindness. If you want to receive gifts, give. If you ask for yourself what you deny to others, your asking is a mockery.

Let this be the pattern for all men when they practice mercy: show mercy to others in the same way, with the same generosity, with the same promptness, as you want others to show mercy to you.

Therefore, let prayer, mercy and fasting be

one single plea to God on our behalf, one speech in our defense, a threefold unity of prayer in our favor.

Let us use fasting to make up for what we have lost by despising others. Let us offer our souls in sacrifice by means of fasting. There is nothing more pleasing that we can offer to God, as the psalmist said in prophecy: "A sacrifice to God is a broken spirit; God does not despise a bruised and humbled heart."

Offer your soul to God, make him an oblation of your fasting, so that your soul may be a pure offering, a holy sacrifice, a living victim, remaining your own and at the same time made over to God. Whoever fails to give this to God will not be excused, for if you are to give him yourself you are never without the means of giving.

To make these acceptable, mercy must be added. Fasting bears no fruit unless it is watered by mercy. Fasting dries up when mercy dries up. Mercy is to fasting as rain is to the earth. However much you may cultivate your heart, clear the soil of your nature, root out vices, sow virtues, if you do not release the springs of mercy, your fasting will bear no fruit.

When you fast, if your mercy is thin your harvest will be thin; when you fast, what you pour out in mercy overflows into your barn. Therefore, do not lose by saving, but gather in by scattering. Give to the poor, and you give to yourself. You will not be allowed to keep what you have refused to give to others.

From a Sermon by Saint Peter Chrysologus

"I appeal to you by the mercy of God." This appeal is made by Paul, or rather, it is made by God through Paul, because of God's desire to be loved rather than feared, to be a father rather than a Lord. God appeals to us in his mercy to avoid having to punish us in his severity.

Listen to the Lord's appeal: In me, I want you to see your own body, your members, your heart, your bones, your blood. You may fear what is divine, but why not love what is human? You may run away from me as the Lord, but why not run to me as your father? Perhaps you are filled with shame for causing my bitter passion. Do not be afraid. This cross inflicts a mortal injury, not on me, but on death. These nails no longer pain me, but only deepen your love for me. I do not cry out because of these wounds, but through them I draw you into my heart. My body was stretched on the cross as a symbol, not of how much I suffered, but of my all-embracing love. I count it no loss to shed my blood: it is the price I have paid for your ransom. Come, then, return to me and learn to know me as your father, who repays good for evil, love for injury, and boundless charity for piercing wounds.

Listen now to what the Apostle urges us to do: "I appeal to you," he says, "to present your bodies as a living sacrifice." By this exhortation of his, Paul has raised all men to priestly status.

How marvelous is the priesthood of the Christian, for he is both the victim that is offered on his own behalf, and the priest who makes the offering. He does not need to go beyond himself to seek what he is to immolate to God: with himself and in himself he brings the sacrifice he is to offer God for himself. The victim remains and the priest remains, always one and the same. Immolated, the victim still lives: the priest who immolates cannot kill. Truly it is an amazing sacrifice in which a body is offered without being slain and blood is offered without being shed.

The Apostle says: "I appeal to you by the mercy of God to present your bodies as a living sacrifice." Brethren, this sacrifice follows the pattern of Christ's sacrifice by which he gave his body as a living immolation for the life of the world. He really made his body a living sacrifice, because, though slain, he continues to live. In such a victim death receives its ransom, but the victim remains alive. Death itself suffers the punishment. This is why death for the martyrs is actually a birth, and their end a beginning. Their execution is the door to life, and those who were thought to have been blotted out from the earth shine brilliantly in heaven.

Paul says: "I appeal to you by the mercy of God to present your bodies as a sacrifice, living and holy." The prophet said the same thing: "Sacrifice and offering you did not desire, but you have prepared a body for me." Each of us is called to be both a sacrifice to God and his priest. Do not forfeit what divine authority confers on you. Put on the garment of holiness, gird yourself with the belt of chastity. Let Christ be your helmet, let the cross on your forehead be your unfailing protection. Your breastplate should be the knowledge of God that he himself has given you. Keep burning continually the sweet-smelling incense of prayer. Take up the sword of the Spirit. Let your heart be an altar. Then, with full confidence in God, present your body for sacrifice. God desires not death, but faith; God thirsts not for blood, but for self-surrender; God is appeased not by slaughter, but by the offering of your free will.

From a Sermon by Saint Peter Chrysologus

The holy Apostle has told us that the human race takes its origin from two men, Adam and Christ; two men equal in body but unequal in merit, wholly alike in their physical structure but totally unlike in the very origin of their being. "The first man, Adam," he says, "became a living soul, the last Adam a life-giving spirit."

The first Adam was made by the last Adam, from whom he also received his soul, to give him life. The last Adam was formed by his own action; he did not have to wait for life to be given him by someone else, but was the only one who could give life to all. The first Adam was formed from valueless clay, the second Adam came forth from the precious womb of the Virgin. In the case of the first Adam, earth was changed into flesh; in the case of the second Adam, flesh was raised up to be God.

What more need be said? The second Adam stamped his image on the first Adam when he created him. That is why he took on himself the role, and the name, of the first Adam, in order that he might not lose what he had made in his own image. The first Adam, the last Adam; the first had a beginning, the last knows no end. The last Adam is indeed the first; as he himself says, "I am the first and the last."

"I am the first," that is, I have no beginning. "I am the last," that is, I have no end. "But what was spiritual," says the Apostle, "did not come first; what was living came first, then what is spiritual." The earth comes before its fruit, but the earth is not so valuable as its fruit. The earth exacts pain and toil; its fruit bestows subsistence and life. The prophet rightly boasted of this fruit: "Our earth has yielded its fruit." What is this fruit? The fruit referred to in another place: "I will place upon your throne one who is the fruit of your body. The first man," says the Apostle, "was made from the earth and belongs to the earth; the second man is from heaven, and belongs to heaven."

"The man made from the earth is the pattern of those who belong to the earth; the man from heaven is the pattern of those who belong to heaven." How is it that these last, though they do not belong to heaven by birth, will yet belong to heaven, men who do not remain what they were by birth but persevere in being what they have become by rebirth? The reason is, brethren, that the heavenly Spirit, by the mysterious infusion of his light, gives fertility to the womb of the virginal font. The Spirit brings forth as men belonging to heaven those whose earthly ancestry brought them forth as men belonging to the earth, and in a condition of wretchedness; he gives them the likeness of their Creator. Now that we are reborn, refashioned in the image of our Creator, we must fulfill what the Apostle commands: "So, as we have worn the likeness of the man of earth, let us also wear the likeness of the man of heaven."

Now that we are reborn in the likeness of our Lord, and have indeed been adopted by God as his children, let us put on the complete image of our Creator so as to be wholly like him, not in the glory that he alone possesses, but in innocence, simplicity, gentleness, patience, humility, mercy, harmony, those qualities in which he chose to become one of us.

CHAPTER 13

SAINT LEO THE GREAT

Perhaps surprisingly, considering the amount of teaching and writing many of our popes have done, only two of them are included among the Doctors of the Church. These two — Pope Leo I and Pope Gregory I — are also the only popes to be called "the Great." There obviously was something about each of them that stood out, and we'll explore that in this chapter and the next.

The fifth century witnessed a change in the prestige of the papacy as popes played more decisive roles in the theological controversies that were rending the Eastern Church. This began with the first pope of the fifth century, Innocent I, who seized every opportunity to assert the primacy of the Roman see. This was a claim made by his predecessors, but not as forcefully as did Innocent. But Leo proved to be even more effective than Innocent, infusing all his policies and pronouncements with the conviction that supreme and universal authority in the Church, bestowed originally on Peter by Christ, had been transmitted to each subsequent bishop of Rome as the apostle's heir.

Other popes, though, were also strong administrators who insisted on the primacy of the papacy. The reason Leo was proclaimed a Doctor of the Church by Pope Benedict XIV in 1754 was because of his writings and sermons. Chief among the writings was his *Tome*, a famous letter he wrote to Archbishop Flavian of Constantinople that expressed the Christian doctrine that Christ had two natures in one person. Ninety-six sermons and one hundred forty-three letters have also come down to us. The Church prizes them so much that excerpts from the sermons are included in the Office of Readings for many of the main feasts on the liturgical calendar — Christmas and Epiphany, for example. Five sermons on the Beatitudes are also included. In all, excerpts from twenty-six of his sermons are in the Office of Readings, the same number as Saint Ambrose's and second only to Saint Augustine's eighty-two.

We have no reliable information about his birth, but it was around the year 400 and probably in Rome. He served as a deacon under Popes Celestine I and Sixtus III and achieved a certain eminence. He corresponded with Archbishop Cyril of Alexandria, who wanted to prevent the pope from recognizing the Church of Jerusalem as a patriarchate, and Cassian dedicated a treatise he wrote against Nestorianism to Leo. In 440 Leo was sent to Gaul on a diplomatic mission for Pope Sixtus, and while he was there the pope died. A deputation went to Gaul and informed Leo that he had been elected to the Chair of Saint Peter, and Leo returned to Rome for his consecration in September of that year. He was pope for twenty-one years, from 440 until his death in 461.

Leo was determined to make the Roman Church a pattern for other churches, so he began his papacy with a series of the sermons for which he is known, instructing his Christians about Catholic doctrine. He discovered that there were many Manichaeans in Rome, some of whom had fled the Vandals in Africa (see chapter on Saint Augustine). He invoked the civil authorities and saw to it that the Manichaeans' books were burned and that they were banished from Rome. He also wrote to the other Italian bishops warning them of the Manichaeans' presence and he preached against their false teachings.

In Spain, the heresy of Priscillianism was making headway among Christians. It combined astrology with the Manichaean teachings about the evil of matter, and it denied both the preexistence and the humanity of Jesus. Leo received a letter from Bishop Turibius of Spain, who enclosed a letter he had been circulating in opposition to this heresy. Leo wrote back with a long refutation of the heresy and described the measures he had taken in Rome against the Manichaeans.

In Gaul, Leo took it upon himself to intervene when Bishop Hilary of Arles began treating his see as a patriarchate, independent of Rome. He obtained from Emperor Valentinian III a rescript recognizing his jurisdiction through the western provinces of the empire and then he confined Hilary to his diocese. In Africa, another part of the world that valued its independence, Leo made rulings on irregularities in elections and other matters. And in Greece he reminded Bishop Anastasius of Thessalonica that all bishops had a right to appeal to Rome about matters connected with their dioceses. Leo was firmly in charge of the Church in the West.

He encountered more difficulties, however, in the East. The Church there was not inclined to accept the pope's claims of papal primacy. In the year 448, Leo received a letter from Abbot Eutyches of Constantinople, complaining that the Nestorian heresy was being revived. A year later he received another letter, which Eutyches had also sent to the patriarchs of Alexandria and Jerusalem, protesting a sentence of excommunication that had been pronounced on him by Archbishop Flavian, the patriarch of Constantinople. Eutyches' appeal was supported by the eastern emperor, Theodosius II.

Leo hadn't heard anything about this from Flavian, so he wrote to him to get his version of the dispute. Flavian sent Leo a copy of the report of the synod at which Eutyches had been condemned. From this it seemed clear to Leo that Eutyches, in his zeal to combat Nestorianism, had fallen into the opposite heresy and was guilty of denying the human nature of Christ. So this is when Leo wrote his letter to Flavian, his famous *Tome*, in which he concisely defined the Catholic doctrine of the Incarnation. He described the two natures of Christ, divine and human, in one person, carefully avoiding both the heresy of Nestorianism on one hand and of Eutychianism, or Monophysitism, on the other.

Emperor Theodosius II, however, had his own plan for dealing with this matter. He called a council at Ephesus in 449, but packed it with Eutyches' supporters, including Archbishop Dioscorus, patriarch of Alexandria, who presided. Pope Leo was not invited but was allowed to send representatives. The representatives, though, spoke only Latin and not only didn't understand what was being said in Greek but couldn't make themselves understood either. Leo had expected that his *Tome* would be read, but it was rejected.

The council turned into a riot. Dioscoros defended Eutyches so vehemently that Leo's representatives called for his banishment from the proceedings. Then, pretending that he was being attacked, Dioscoros shouted for the imperial commissioner. Suddenly the doors were thrown open and military police and a crowd of thugs rushed in. Dioscoros demanded that all 170 bishops present sign a form rehabilitating Eutyches and deposing his accusers, including Patriarch Flavian.

Then the emperor adjourned the council.

If Emperor Theodosius thought that was the end of the affair, he didn't realize with whom he was dealing in Pope Leo. Leo declared that supreme and universal authority in the Church resided solely in the Bishop of Rome and he refused to recognize the council's proceedings. He wrote to Emperor Theodosius demanding that he call another council to right the injustices of the "robber synod." The emperor ignored him.

Theodosius died in 450 and the new emperor, Marcion, was persuaded to call a new council in Chalcedon, directly across the Bosphorus from Constantinople. The fourth ecumenical council, it convened on October 8, 451. Emperor Marcion thought that the pope, rather than the emperor, should preside at councils, and he invited Pope Leo to do so. Leo did not make the trip from Rome to Chalcedon but he was technically the council's president. The council was attended by six hundred or more bishops.

The Council of Chalcedon reversed the decisions made at Ephesus in 449 (that council is not listed among the Church's councils); tried Dioscoros for what he did at Ephesus and found him guilty; stripped him of his bishopric and the exercise of his ordination; and condemned the teachings of Eutyches. Pope Leo's representatives read Leo's *Tome* that asserted that "he who became man in the form of a servant is he who in the form of God created man." The council members exclaimed, "Peter has spoken by the mouth of Leo!" The Nicene Creed, including what was added at the Council of Constantinople, was read and the council formulated the statement of faith that the Catholic Church still accepts today.

Having settled this doctrinal matter, the council went on to pass a number of canons, the twenty-eighth of which granted Constantinople the same patriarchal status as Rome on the ground that both were imperial cities. Leo refused to accept that canon and declined to approve the council's proceedings until 453. Then he declared canon twenty-eight invalid because it contradicted the canons of the First Council of Nicaea.

Meanwhile, Leo was having other problems back in Rome. In 452, Attila had overrun Greece and Germany with his Huns, was conquering the northern cities of Italy, and was approaching Rome. Emperor Valentinian III was safe in Ravenna. Leo, then, set out with the city's governor and a band of priests and met Attila near where the Po and Mincio rivers meet. Leo managed to convince Attila that he should spare Rome by offering him an annual tribute.

He wasn't able to do quite as well three years later, when Genseric and his Vandals from Africa appeared before Rome's walls. Leo went out to meet him, just as he had done with Attila, but this time he was able only to get a promise that the

Vandals wouldn't burn the city or massacre its residents. They pillaged the city for fifteen days and took back to Africa a host of captives and immense booty.

The Church celebrates his feast on November 10.

Excerpts from the *Tome*, by Saint Leo the Great

Without detriment to the properties of either nature and substance (the divine and the human), which then came together in one person, majesty took on humility, strength weakness, eternity mortality, and for the payment of the debt belonging to our condition inviolable nature was united with suffering nature, so that, as suited the needs of our case, one and the same Mediator between God and men, the Man Jesus Christ, could both die with the one and not die with the other. Thus in the whole and perfect nature of true man was true God born, complete in what was his own, complete in what was ours....

There enters then these lower parts of the world the Son of God, descending from his heavenly home and yet not quitting his Father's glory, begotten in a new order by a new birthing. In a new order, because being invisible in his own nature, he became visible in ours, and he whom nothing could contain was content to be contained. Abiding before all time, he began to be in time; the Lord of all things he obscured his immeasurable majesty and took on himself the form of a servant. Being God who cannot suffer, he did not disdain to be man that can and, immortal as he is, to subject himself to the laws of death.

The Lord assumed his mother's nature without faultiness, nor in the Lord Jesus Christ, born of the Virgin's womb, does the marvel of his birth make his nature unlike ours. For he who is true God is also true man, and in this union there is no deceit, since the humility of manhood and the loftiness of the Godhead both meet there. For as God is not changed by the showing of pity, so man is not swallowed up in the dignity of the Godhead....

To be hungry and thirsty, to be weary and to sleep is clearly human, but to satisfy five thousand men with five loaves, to bestow on the woman of Samaria living water, draughts of which can secure the drinker from thirsting ever again, to walk upon the surface of the water with feet that do not sink and to quell the rising of the waves by rebuking the winds is without any doubt divine.

Just as also — to pass over many other instances — it is not part of the same nature to be moved to tears of pity for a dead friend and, when the stone that closed the four-days grave was removed, to raise that same friend to life with a voice of command; or to hang on the cross, and to turn day into night to make all the elements tremble; or to be pierced with nails and then to open the gates of paradise to the robber's faith. So it is not part of the same nature to say: "I and the Father are one," and to say: "The Father is greater than I." For although in the Lord Jesus Christ God and man is one person, yet the source of the degradation which is shared by both is one, and the source of the glory which is shared by both is another. For his manhood, which is less than the Father, comes from our side; his Godhead, which is equal to the Father, comes from the Father.

From a Christmas Sermon, by Saint Leo the Great

Dearly beloved, today our Savior is born; let us rejoice. Sadness should have no place on the birthday of life. The fear of death has been swallowed up; life brings us joy with the promise of eternal happiness.

No one is shut out from this joy; all share the same reason for rejoicing. Our Lord, victor over sin and death, finding no man free from sin, came to free us all. Let the saint rejoice as he sees the palm of victory at hand. Let the sinner be glad as he receives the offer of forgiveness. Let the pagan take courage as he is summoned to life.

In the fullness of time, chosen in the unfathomable depths of God's wisdom, the Son of God took for himself our common humanity in order to reconcile it with its creator. He came to overthrow the devil, the origin of death, in that very nature by which he had overthrown mankind.

And so at the birth of our Lord the angels sing in joy: "Glory to God in the highest," and they proclaim peace "to his people on earth" as they see the heavenly Jerusalem being built from all the nations of the world. When the angels on high are so exultant at this marvelous work of God's goodness, what joy should it not bring to the lowly hearts of men?

Beloved, let us give thanks to God the Father, through his Son, in the Holy Spirit, because in his great love for us he took pity on us, "and when we were dead in our sins he brought us to life with Christ," so that in him we might be a new creation. Let us throw off our old nature and all its ways and, as we have come to birth in Christ, let us renounce the works of the flesh.

Christian, remember your dignity, and now that you share in God's own nature, do not return by sin to your former base condition. Bear in mind who is your head and of whose body you are a member. Do not forget that you have been rescued from the power of darkness and brought into the light of God's kingdom.

Through the sacrament of baptism you have become a temple of the Holy Spirit. Do not drive away so great a guest by evil conduct and become again a slave to the devil, for your liberty was bought by the blood of Christ.

From a Sermon by Saint Leo the Great

Beloved, I am both weak and lazy in fulfilling the obligations of my office; whenever I try to act with vigor and devotedness, the frailty of our human condition slows me down. Yet I share in the ever-present atoning work of that almighty and eternal high priest, who is like us and yet equal to the Father; he brought the Godhead down to our human level and raised our humanity to the Godhead. Rightly, then, do we rejoice in what he established; for, though he delegated to many shepherds the care of his sheep, he has not ceased to watch over in person the flock that is dear to him.

It is from this ultimate, inexhaustible source of security that we have received strength in our apostolic task; for his activity is never relaxed. The powerful foundation upon which the whole structure of the Church rests is never shaken by the weight of the temple that presses upon it.

That faith which Christ commended in the prince of the apostles remains forever unshaken. And, just as Peter's faith in Christ endures, so does

Christ's foundation upon Peter. The structure of truth persists; blessed Peter retains his rock-like strength and has not abandoned the helm of the Church which he took over.

Peter is call the rock; he is declared to be the foundation; he is made doorkeeper of the heavenly kingdom; he is made judge of what is to be bound or loosed, and his judgments remain valid even in heaven; in these various ways, he is assigned a rank above the others. By reflecting on the hidden meaning of these titles of his, we can come to appreciate how close he is to Christ.

In our day he carries out his trust over a wider field and with greater power; he attends to every department of his duties and responsibilities in and along with him who gave him that dignity.

And so, if I do anything well, if my judgment is sound, if I obtain anything from God's mercy by my daily prayer, all this is due to the achievement and the deserts of Peter; it is his power that lives on in his see, it is his prestige that reigns.

This, beloved, is the outcome of that profession of faith which God the Father inspired in the Apostle's heart. That declaration rose above the doubts of all merely human opinion, and took on the solidity of a rock unshaken by any outside pressure.

For, in the world-wide Church, every day Peter declares: "You are the Christ, the Son of the living God," and every man who acknowledges the

Lord is enabled to proclaim what those words mean.

From a Sermon by Saint Leo the Great

My dear brethren, there is no doubt that the Son of God took our human nature into so close a union with himself that one and the same Christ is present, not only in the firstborn of all creation, but in all his saints as well. The head cannot be separated from the members, nor the members from the head. Not in this life, it is true, but only in eternity will God be all in all, yet even now he dwells, whole and undivided, in his temple the Church. Such was his promise to us when he said: "See, I am with you always, even to the end of the world."

And so all that the Son of God did and taught for the world's reconciliation is not for us simply a matter of past history. Here and now we experience his power at work among us. Born of a virgin mother by the action of the Holy Spirit, Christ keeps his Church spotless and makes her fruitful by the inspiration of the same Spirit. In baptismal regeneration she brings forth children for God beyond all numbering. These are the sons of whom it is written: "They are born not of blood, nor of the desire of the flesh, nor of the will of man, but of God."

In Christ Abraham's posterity is blessed, because in him the whole world receives the adoption of sons, and in him the patriarch becomes the father of all nations through the birth, not from human stock but by faith, of the descendants that were promised to him. From every nation on earth, without exception, Christ forms a single flock of those he has sanctified, daily fulfilling the promise he once made: "I have other sheep, not of this fold, whom it is also ordained that I shall lead; and there shall be one flock and one shepherd."

Although it was primarily to Peter that he said: "Feed my sheep," yet the one Lord guides all pastors in the discharge of their office and leads to rich and fertile pastures all those who come to the rock. There is no counting the sheep who are nourished with his abundant love, and who are prepared to lay down their lives for the sake of the good shepherd who died for them.

But it is not only the martyrs who share in his passion by their glorious courage; the same is true, by faith, of all who are born again in baptism. That is why we are to celebrate the Lord's paschal sacrifice with the unleavened bread of sincerity and truth. The leaven of our former malice is thrown out, and a new creature is filled and inebriated with the Lord himself. For the effect of our sharing in the body and blood of Christ is to change us into what we receive. As we have died with him, and have been buried and raised to life with him, so we bear him within us, both in body and in spirit, in everything we do.

CHAPTER 14

SAINT GREGORY THE GREAT

One hundred twenty-nine years, from 461 to 590, separate the papacies of Pope Leo I and Pope Gregory I — the only two popes who are called "the Great" and the only two popes who have been declared Doctors of the Church. In addition, Pope Gregory earned recognition as one of the great Fathers of the Western Church along with Saints Ambrose, Augustine, and Jerome. He has been called the father of the medieval papacy.

A lot happened in the century and a quarter between the two "great" popes — and not much of it good. The barbarian tribes overran Italy not long after Leo the Great's death and the line of western emperors came to an end in 476. After that the barbarian Odoacer ruled Italy from Ravenna. In 493, another barbarian, the Arian Theodoric, at the bidding of eastern Emperor Zeno, captured Rome and Ravenna, killed Odoacer and installed himself in Ravenna as vice-emperor. But the Ostrogoths continued to fight the imperial forces from Constantinople for control of Italy. In 535, Emperor Justinian, who had already taken North

Africa from the Vandals who had occupied it since Saint Augustine's last days, fought against the Ostrogoths. Wars lasted from 535 to 553, when the Gothic kingdom in Italy came to an end. After that the emperor in Constantinople ruled Italy by an exarch who lived in Ravenna. Rome, once the greatest city in the world, was in ruins after being conquered four times in twenty years. According to the historian Procopius, at one point only five hundred people lived in the city. There was anarchy.

This was the situation when Gregory was born in Rome about the year 540. Although he was born into a wealthy family — his family owned large estates in Sicily as well as a magnificent home on the Caelian Hill in Rome — as a boy he lived through the horrors of a siege when Romans had no food. Besides being wealthy, his family was also known for its piety, having already given to the Church two sixth-century popes, Felix III and Agapitus I.

It's not clear how children were educated amid the turmoil of Rome in those days, but somehow Gregory received a good education. He studied law and prepared to follow his father into public service. By the age of thirty, he was appointed prefect of Rome, the highest civil office in the city. When his father died, and his mother retired to a convent, Gregory was one of the richest men in Rome.

Then he gave it all up. He abandoned his career in order to devote himself to the service of God. He went to Sicily where he turned his estates into six monasteries. Then he returned to Rome, made his own home into a Benedictine monastery under the patronage of Saint Andrew, and became one of the monks there.

He remained a simple monk for three or four years before Pope Pelagius II appointed him a deacon, which meant a more active life outside the monastery. Rome was then once again being besieged, this time by the Lombards, and the pope sent Gregory to Constantinople as a papal ambassador to beg for military aid from the new emperor, Tiberias II. He was unsuccessful in his mission because the emperor insisted that his troops were too busy fending off the Persians and other enemies.

Gregory remained in Constantinople for about six years. Here he saw the contrast between the magnificence of the present imperial city of Constantinople and the misery of the former imperial city of Rome. He was at a disadvantage in his role as ambassador since he knew no Greek and he spent most of his time living a monastic life with several monks from Saint Andrew's that he brought with him. He also began to write a mystical and allegorical commentary on the Book of Job, called *Moral Reflections on Job,* which he completed after he became pope. While in Constantinople, too, he became an expert on the Eastern Church, which was to serve him well in later years. He was recalled to Rome in 586 and moved back into Saint Andrew's Monastery, where he was soon elected abbot. He also served as a confidential adviser to Pope Pelagius.

It was during this period of his life that Gregory became interested in the reconversion of England. Receiving the approval of the pope, he set out with several monks in the direction of England. But when the people of Rome learned that their favorite cleric was leaving, they raised such an outcry that the pope sent envoys to bring the party back.

An outbreak of the plague racked Rome in 590 and Pope Pelagius was one of its victims. The general consensus was that Gregory was the most qualified man to succeed him and, pending Emperor Maurice's approval, he carried on the government of the Church. But he also wrote a letter to the emperor imploring him not to give his approval. The prefect of Rome, though, intercepted Gregory's letter and wrote one of his own, telling the emperor that the popular vote for Gregory was unanimous. Emperor Maurice promptly ratified the election and Gregory was consecrated pope on September 3, 590. He was about fifty years old and he was the first monk to be elected pope.

Early in his pontificate, after being mildly censured by Archbishop John of Ravenna for trying to avoid his office, Gregory wrote one of his most important works — the *Regula Pastoralis*, or *Pastoral Guide*, a book on the responsibilities of a bishop. He wrote that a bishop should first of all be a physician of souls whose chief duties are preaching and the enforcement of discipline. It was an immediate success. Emperor Maurice had it translated into Greek, and Bishop Leander of Spain into Spanish. Three hundred years after it was written, King Albert of England had it translated into Anglo-Saxon. In the ninth century, Charlemagne ordered all bishops to study it and to give a copy to every new bishop as part of the ceremony of consecration.

Gregory proceeded to write *Dialogues*, an account of the lives and miracles of saints, including a life of Saint Benedict of Nursia, the founder of the Benedictine Order. Of his other writings, forty short homilies on the Gospels, twenty-two longer homilies on Ezekiel, two homilies on the Song of Songs, part of a commentary on the First Book of Samuel, and about eight hundred fifty letters survive.

Gregory was a strong administrator. He conducted a massive reform of the clergy, enforcing the celibacy of the clergy and removing unworthy priests from office. He promoted monasticism and appointed many monks to prominent positions. He emptied the Church's treasury by launching a series of charitable programs to feed the large numbers of hungry people throughout Italy, and he reorganized the Patrimony of Peter, the vast lands owned by the papacy.

He was particularly interested in the liturgy. About eighty prayers in what later was called the Gregorian Sacramentary are attributed to him, although the sacramentary itself wasn't finished until about 630. Gregorian Chant is also named after him although Gregory's actual role in its development is questioned.

Of all his work as pope, though, nothing was more dear to him than the conversion of England. Here he turned to his own monastery and chose a band of forty monks, under the leadership of the man who has gone down in history as Saint Augustine of Canterbury, to proceed to England. He instructed the monks to purify rather than destroy pagan temples and customs, and to take over pagan rites and festivals and turn them into Christian feasts. Although Augustine himself died only eight years after he arrived in England, the work he began there eventually bore fruit.

Gregory was pope for thirteen years. During nearly all of those years he was in conflict with either the emperor or the patriarch in Constantinople. The patriarch, John Faster, assumed the title of Ecumenical Patriarch, and Gregory objected, charging that the title smacked of arrogance and seemed to challenge the pope's supremacy. John replied that his claim was simply that he was archbishop over many bishops. Emperor Maurice rebuked Gregory for making a fuss over a title, but Gregory argued that Saint Peter's commission from Jesus made all churches, Constantinople included, subject to Rome. Gregory himself, although he acted with authority, preferred the title Servant of the Servants of God, one of the titles retained by his successors.

From the very start of his pontificate, Gregory had to fill the vacuum that existed in the civil government of Rome. The Lombards were constantly threatening the city. Gregory, therefore, organized the city's defenses. In 593 Lombard King Agilulph appeared before the city's walls and it was Gregory who went out to negotiate with him, just as Pope Leo the Great had done with Attila and Genseric. Agilulph withdrew his army.

Gregory ransomed captives from the Lombards and for nine years tried to bring about a peace settlement between Emperor Maurice and King Agilulph. When an agreement was finally reached, it was wrecked by the treachery of the exarch in Ravenna, so Gregory negotiated his own truce for Rome and the surrounding area. Agilulph's wife, Theodelinda, a Bavarian princess, was a Catholic and an ally of Gregory. She managed to prevail on the Lombards to give up Arianism and to accept Catholicism.

Throughout his life, Gregory practiced asceticism. His health was always precarious. He suffered from gastric disorders, probably caused by excessive fasting. During the last years of his life he was emaciated almost to a skeleton. He suffered from gout and was unable to walk at the time of his death. He died on March 12, 604 and was buried in Saint Peter's Basilica in Rome.

The Church celebrates his feast on September 3.

From *Pastoral Guide*, by Saint Gregory the Great

A spiritual guide should be silent when discretion requires and speak when words are of service. Otherwise he may say what he should not or be silent when he should speak. Indiscreet speech may lead men into error and an imprudent silence may leave in error those who could have been taught. Pastors who lack foresight hesitate to say openly what is right because they fear losing the favor of men. As the voice of truth tells us, such leaders are not zealous pastors who protect their flocks, rather they are like mercenaries who flee by taking refuge in silence when the wolf appears.

The Lord reproaches them through the prophet: "They are dumb dogs that cannot bark." On another occasion he complains: "You did not advance against the foe or set up a wall in front of the house of Israel, so that you might stand fast in battle on the day of the Lord." To advance against the foe involves a bold resistance to the powers of this world in defense of the flock. To stand fast in battle on the day of the Lord means to oppose the wicked enemy out of love for what is right.

When a pastor has been afraid to assert what is right, has he not turned his back and fled by remaining silent? Whereas if he intervenes on behalf of the flock, he sets up a wall against the enemy in front of the house of Israel. Therefore, the Lord again says to his unfaithful people: "Your prophets saw false and foolish visions and did not point out your wickedness, that you might repent of your sins." The name of prophet is sometimes given in the sacred writings to teachers who both declare the present to be fleeting and reveal what is to come. The word of God accuses them of seeing false visions because they are afraid to reproach men for their faults and thereby lull the evildoer with an empty promise of safety. Because they fear reproach, they keep silent and fail to point out the sinner's wrongdoing.

The word of reproach is a key that unlocks a door, because reproach reveals a fault of which the evildoer is himself often unaware. That is why Paul says of the bishop: "He must be able to encourage men in sound doctrine and refute those who oppose it." For the same reason God tells us through Malachi: "The lips of the priest are to preserve knowledge, and men shall look to him for the law, for he is the messenger of the Lord of hosts." Finally, that is also the reason why the Lord warns us through Isaiah: "Cry out and be not still; raise your voice in a trumpet call."

Anyone ordained a priest undertakes the task of preaching, so that with a loud cry he may go on ahead of the terrible judge who follows. If, then, a priest does not know how to preach, what kind of cry can such a dumb herald utter? It was to bring this home that the Holy Spirit descended in the form of tongues on the first pastors, for he causes those whom he has filled, to speak out spontaneously.

From *Moral Reflections on Job*, by Saint Gregory the Great

Holy Job is a type of the Church. At one point he speaks for the body, at another for the head. As he speaks of its members he is suddenly caught up to speak in the name of their head. So it is where he says: "I have suffered this without sin on my hands, for my prayer to God was pure."

Christ suffered without sin on his hands, for he committed no sin and deceit was not found on his lips. Yet he suffered the pain of the cross for our redemption. His prayer to God was pure, his alone out of all mankind, for in the midst of his suffering he prayed for his persecutors: "Father, forgive them, for they do not know what they are doing."

Is it possible to offer, or even to imagine, a purer kind of prayer than that which shows mercy to one's torturers by making intercession for them? It was thanks to this kind of prayer that the frenzied persecutors who shed the blood of our Redeemer drank it afterward in faith and proclaimed him to be the Son of God.

The text goes on fittingly to speak of Christ's blood: "Earth, do not cover over my blood, do not let my cry find a hiding place in you." When man sinned, God had said: "Earth you are, and to earth you will return." Earth does not cover over the blood of our Redeemer, for every sinner, as he drinks the blood that is the price of his redemption, offers praise and thanksgiving, and to the best of his power makes that blood known to all around him.

Earth has not hidden away his blood, for holy Church has preached in every corner of the world the mystery of its redemption.

Notice what follows: "Do not let my cry find a hiding place in you." The blood that is drunk, the blood of redemption, is itself the cry of our Redeemer. Paul speaks of "the sprinkled blood that calls out more eloquently than Abel's." Of Abel's blood Scripture had written: "The voice of your brother's blood cries out to me from the earth."

The blood of Jesus calls out more eloquently than Abel's, for the blood of Abel asked for the death of Cain the fratricide, while the blood of the Lord has asked for, and obtained, life for his persecutors.

If the sacrament of the Lord's passion is to work its effect in us, we must imitate what we receive and proclaim to mankind what we revere. The cry of the Lord finds a hiding place in us if our lips fail to speak of this, though our hearts believe in it. So that his cry may not lie concealed in us it remains for us all, each in his own measure, to make known to those around us the mystery of our new life in Christ.

From *Dialogues*, by Saint Gregory the Great

Scholastica, the sister of Saint Benedict, had been consecrated to God from her earliest years. She was accustomed to visiting her brother once a year. He would come down to meet her at a place on the monastery property, not far outside the gate.

One day she came as usual and her saintly brother went with some of his disciples; they spent the whole day praising God and talking of sacred things. As night fell they had supper together.

Their spiritual conversation went on and the hour grew late. The holy nun said to her brother: "Please do not leave me tonight; let us go on until morning talking about the delights of the spiritual life."

"Sister," he replied, "what are you saying? I simply cannot stay outside my cell."

When she heard her brother refuse her request, the holy woman joined her hands on the table, laid her head on them and began to pray. As she raised her head from the table, there were such brilliant flashes of lightning, such great peals of thunder and such a heavy downpour of rain that neither Benedict nor his brethren could stir across the threshold of the place where they had been seated.

Sadly he began to complain: "May God forgive you, sister. What have you done?"

"Well," she answered, "I asked you and you would not listen; so I asked my God and he did listen. So now go off, if you can, leave me and return to your monastery."

Reluctant as he was to stay of his own will, he remained against his will. So it came about that they stayed awake the whole night, engrossed in their conversation about the spiritual life.

It is not surprising that she was more effective than he; since, as John says, "God is love," it was absolutely right that she could do more, as she loved more.

Three days later, Benedict was in his cell. Looking up to the sky, he saw his sister's soul leave her body in the form of a dove, and fly up to the secret places of heaven. Rejoicing in her great glory, he thanked almighty God with hymns and words of praise. He then sent his brethren to bring her body to the monastery and lay it in the tomb he had prepared for himself.

Their minds had always been united in God; their bodies were to share a common grave.

From a Homily on the Gospels, by Saint Gregory the Great

"I am the good shepherd. I know my own" — by which I mean, I love them — "and my own know me." In plain words: those who love me are willing to follow me, for anyone who does not love the truth has not yet come to know it.

My dear brethren, you have heard the test we pastors have to undergo. Turn now to consider how these words of our Lord imply a test for yourselves also. Ask yourselves whether you belong to his flock, whether you know him, whether the light of his truth shines in your minds. I assure you that it is not by faith that you will come to know him, but by love; not by mere conviction, but by action. John the evangelist is my authority for this statement. He tells us that "anyone who claims to know God without keeping his commandments is a liar."

Consequently, the Lord immediately adds:

"As the Father knows me and I know the Father; and I lay down my life for my sheep." Clearly he means that laying down his life for his sheep gives evidence of his knowledge of the Father and the Father's knowledge of him. In other words, by the love with which he dies for his sheep he shows how greatly he loves his Father.

Again he says: "My sheep hear my voice, and I know them; they follow me, and I give them eternal life." Shortly before this he had declared: "If anyone enters the sheepfold through me he shall be saved; he shall go freely in and out and shall find good pasture." He will enter into a life of faith; from faith he will go out to vision, from belief to contemplation, and will graze in the good pastures of everlasting life.

So our Lord's sheep will finally reach their grazing ground where all who follow him in simplicity of heart will feed on the green pastures of eternity. These pastures are the spiritual joys of heaven. There the elect look upon the face of God with unclouded vision and feast at the banquet of life forever more.

Beloved brothers, let us set out for these pastures where we shall keep joyful festival with so many of our fellow citizens. May the thought of their happiness urge us on! Let us stir up our hearts, rekindle our faith, and long eagerly for what heaven has in store for us. To love thus is to be already on our way. No matter what obstacles we encounter, we must not allow them to turn us aside from the joy of that heavenly feast. Anyone who is determined to reach his destination is not deterred by the roughness of the road that leads to it. Nor must we allow the charm of success to seduce us, or we shall be like a foolish traveler who is so distracted by the pleasant meadows through which he is passing that he forgets where he is going.

Chapter 15

SAINT ISIDORE OF SEVILLE

Saint Isidore of Seville is the first of three Spaniards to be declared Doctors of the Church, and he lived almost a millennium before the other two — Saints Teresa of Avila and John of the Cross. He is usually referred to as Isidore of Seville to distinguish him from another Spanish saint, Isidore the Farmer, who died in 1130.

The Europe of the latter part of the sixth century and the first part of the seventh, when Isidore lived, was divided among various Teutonic barbarian tribes: the Lombards in Italy, the Visigoths in Spain, the Franks in Gaul, and the Anglo-Saxons in Britain. In Spain, the Visigoths had been Arian until the Third Council of Toledo in 589 when King Recared accepted the Catholic faith for all of Spain.

Isidore was born into a pious family about the year 560. Two of his brothers, Leander and Fulgentius, like Isidore, became bishops and saints, and one of his sisters, Florentina, was an abbess of many convents and later declared a saint. After their parents' deaths, Isidore was entrusted to his brother Leander, who was twenty-six years older than Isidore and a Benedictine monk.

Leander was a severe and demanding teacher and sometimes Isidore rebelled. The anecdote is told about Isidore's running away from school one day. As he sat by himself in a woods, he watched some drops of water falling on a rock. Then he noticed that the dripping water had worn a hole in the rock. This made him think that he could do what the drops of water did, that little by little he could learn all his brother demanded. He went on to become the best scholar and the most learned man of his time, mastering Latin, Greek and Hebrew as well as theology and the other liberal arts.

Leander became the bishop of Seville when Isidore was a young man, and Isidore assisted his brother in administering the diocese. They began the successful organization of the Spanish Church and established a school for the teaching of religion, art, and science that became a model for schools in other Spanish sees. Leander was an evangelist to the Visigoths. He presided at the Third Council of Toledo at which the Visigoths renounced Arianism and accepted Catholicism.

Leander died in 601 and Isidore succeeded him as bishop of Seville. He completed the work he and Leander had begun of converting the Visigoths. He also continued Leander's practice of settling the Church's disciplinary matters, and promoting theological and ecclesiastical unity, in the

Spanish Church through regional councils. He presided over the Second Council of Seville in 619 and the Fourth Council of Toledo in 633. At the latter council he was given preference over the archbishop of Toledo out of respect for his age by that time and his accomplishments as the greatest teacher in Spain.

Isidore didn't teach only the classical curriculum popular in his time, but embraced every known branch of knowledge. His schools taught the liberal arts, medicine, other sciences, and law as well as Hebrew and Greek. He is credited with introducing the philosophy of Aristotle in Spanish schools long before the Muslim Arabs did so after their conquest of Spain and still longer before Saint Thomas Aquinas did so in other parts of Europe in the thirteenth century.

Isidore was a voluminous writer. His writings form the earliest chapter of Spanish literature. Perhaps his most important contribution to education was the compilation of an encyclopedia called *Etymologies* or *Origins*, a summary of all the knowledge of his age. Although outdated today, it was one of the most widely used texts of the Middle Ages and continued to be used for nine centuries. This encyclopedia earned him the title "The Schoolmaster of the Middle Ages" and one of his contemporaries called him "the man who saved Spain from barbarism."

But *Etymologies* was only a small part of his

literary output. His earlier works included a *Dictionary of Synonyms*, a treatise on astronomy and physical geography, a history of the principal events of the world from creation to the year 615, a manual of Christian doctrine, a biography of illustrious men, a book of Old and New Testament personalities, and *The History of the Kings of the Goths, Vandals, and Suevi* (our best source book for the early history of Spain).

He also wrote, at the request of religious orders, a code of rules for monks which bore his name and was generally followed throughout Spain. He wrote extensive theological and ecclesiastical works. And he completed the Mozarabic missal and breviary which his brother Leander had begun to adapt for the use of the Goths, a liturgy that is still in use in Toledo, Spain.

Besides his learning, Isidore was, of course, recognized and admired for his sanctity. When he felt that his life on earth was about to end, he asked two bishops to visit him. The three men went into the church where one of the bishops covered him with sackcloth while the other put ashes on his head. Isidore then raised his hands toward heaven and prayed aloud for the forgiveness of his sins. He then received the last sacraments of the Church, asked those present for their prayers, forgave his debtors, and distributed all of his possessions to the poor. He then returned to his house where he died peacefully shortly thereafter in 636 at about the age of seventy-six.

He was canonized in 1598 by Pope Clement VIII and declared a Doctor of the Church in 1722 by Pope Innocent XIII. His feast is celebrated on April 4.

From the *Book of Maxims*, by Saint Isidore

Prayer purifies us, reading instructs us. Both are good when both are possible. Otherwise, prayer is better than reading.

If a man wants to be always in God's company, he must pray regularly and read regularly. When we pray, we talk to God; when we read, God talks to us.

All spiritual growth comes from reading and reflection. By reading we learn what we did not know; by reflection we retain what we have learned.

Reading the holy Scriptures confers two benefits. It trains the mind to understand them; it turns man's attention from the follies of the world and leads them to the love of God.

Two kinds of study are called for here. We must first learn how the Scriptures are to be understood, and then see how to expound them with profit and in a manner worthy of them. A man must first be eager to understand what he is reading before he is fit to proclaim what he has learned.

The conscientious reader will be more concerned to carry out what he has read than merely to acquire knowledge of it. For it is a less serious fault to be ignorant of an objective than it is to fail to carry out what we do know. In reading we aim at knowing, but we must put into practice what we have learned in our course of study.

No one can understand holy Scripture without constant reading, according to the words: "Love her and she will exalt you. Embrace her and she will glorify you."

The more you devote yourself to a study of the sacred utterances, the richer will be your understanding of them, just as the more the soil is tilled, the richer the harvest.

Some people have great mental powers but cannot be bothered with reading; what reading could have taught them is devalued by their neglect. Others have a desire to know but are hampered by their slow mental processes; yet application to reading will teach them things which the clever fail to learn through laziness.

The man who is slow to grasp things but who really tries hard is rewarded; equally he who does not cultivate his God-given intellectual ability is condemned for despising his gifts and sinning by sloth.

Learning unsupported by grace may get into our ears; it never reaches the heart. It makes a great noise outside but serves no inner purpose. But when God's grace touches our innermost minds to bring understanding, his word which has been received by the ear sinks deep into the heart.

CHAPTER 16

SAINT BEDE

This saint has long been known popularly as "the Venerable Bede," a term of respect bestowed on him in 836 by the Council of Aix-la-Chapelle (or Aachen). Although he was canonized a saint, "Venerable," — which today is the title of one who has reached the first step in the canonization process — seems to remain his special designation.

If, as I said in the first chapter of this volume, Saint Athanasius probably lived the most tumultuous life of all the Doctors of the Church, Saint Bede probably lived the most peaceful. He spent almost his entire life, from the age of seven, in the Benedictine monastery of Saints Peter and Paul at Wearmouth-Jarrow, on the River Tyne in northeastern England. He had even been born on the lands of that monastery in 673.

Almost all we know about Bede's life comes from the last chapter of his greatest work, *Historia Ecclesiastica*, an ecclesiastical history of England, a work that he completed in 729. His parents gave him to Abbot Benedict when he was seven to be educated in the monastery. He became an extraordinary scholar, well-versed in all the sciences of his times: natural philosophy, astronomy, arithmetic, grammar, the philosophy of Aristotle, the lives of saints, and history. He became recognized as probably the most learned man of Western Europe of his era.

He wrote in *Historia Ecclesiastica*, "Through all the observance of monastic discipline, it has ever been my delight to learn and teach and write." He passed his life at the monastery at Jarrow with a monk's regular routine of prayer and praise, study and writing.

Bede was ordained to the diaconate when he was nineteen and to the priesthood when he was thirty. He wrote, "From the time of my ordination up till my present fifty-ninth year I have endeavored for my own use and for that of the brethren to make brief notes upon the holy Scriptures, either out of the works of the venerable fathers or in conformity with their meaning and interpretation."

He has been called "the Father of English History" for his *Historia Ecclesiastica*. Other historians consider it a monumental achievement, thorough and scholarly. The late English Cardinal Gasquet wrote: "Reflect how this great record of our own country was composed. Remember that its author was a man who lived his whole life within the narrow circuit of a few miles. Remember also the difficulty of obtaining information in those days. Still, to acquire knowledge, accurate knowledge, he went to work precisely as the historian would at the present day, never resting till he had got at the best sources of information available at the cost of whatever time or patience or labor it might involve. It is only now, in this age of minute criticism, that we can realize the full excellence of Bede's historical methods. The chief study of St. Bede and his fellow monks at Wearmouth and Jarrow was the Bible. It was from this monastery that has come to us the most correct manuscript of the Vulgate, a scientific achievement of the highest quality."

Historia Ecclesiastica, however, was not Bede's only work. In all, he wrote forty- five books, thirty of which were commentaries on the Gospels, Acts of the Apostles, and other parts of both the Old and New Testaments. He produced a scientific study based on the Roman writers Pliny the Younger and Suetonius, a biography of St. Cuthbert, and a history of the lives of the abbots of Wearmouth and Jarrow.

It was Bede who began dating time from the birth of Christ as A.D. (*Anno Domini*) in his books *De Temporibus* (*On Time*) and *De Temporum Ratione* (*On the Reckoning of Time*).

Bede not only wrote his own books but he copied and translated books by other authors. He also taught the younger monks and supervised them while they copied the Bible and other works.

Bede began to experience the symptoms of his last illness about ten days before Easter in 735. Nevertheless, during the forty days between Easter and Ascension he dictated two new books, one a translation of St. John's Gospel into Anglo-Saxon and the other a collection of notes from Saint Isidore of Seville. He died on Ascension Eve in 735 at age 62. (An account of his death, which is included in the Office of Readings on his feast, follows this paragraph.) He was canonized and declared a Doctor of the Church by Pope Leo XIII in 1899, the only Doctor from England. The Church celebrates his feast, which he shares with Saint Gregory VII and Saint Mary Magdalene de Pazzi, on May 25.

From a Letter on the Death of Bede, by Cuthbert

On Tuesday before the feast of the Ascension, Bede's breathing became labored and a slight swelling appeared in his legs. Nevertheless, he gave us instruction all day long and dictated cheerfully during the whole time. Among other things he repeated several times: "Learn your lesson quickly, for I do not know how long I shall be with you nor whether my Maker will soon take me from you." It seemed to us, however, that he knew very well that his end was near, and so he spent the whole night giving thanks to God.

At daybreak on Wednesday he told us to finish the writing we had begun. We worked until nine o'clock, when we went in procession with the relics as the custom of that day required. But one of our community, a boy named Wilbert, stayed with him and said to him: "Dear master, there is still one more chapter to finish in that book you were dictating. Do you think it would be too hard for you to answer any more questions?"

Bede replied: "Not at all; it will be easy. Take up your pen and ink, and write quickly," and he did so.

At three o'clock, Bede said to me: "I have a few treasures in my private chest, some pepper, napkins, and a little incense. Run quickly and bring the priests of our monastery, and I will distribute among them these little presents that God has given me."

When the priests arrived he spoke to them and asked each one to offer Masses and prayers for him regularly. They gladly promised to do so. The priests were sad, however, and they all wept, especially because Bede had said that he thought they would not see his face much longer in this world. Yet they rejoiced when he said: "If it so please my Maker, it is time for me to return to him who created me and formed me out of nothing when I did not exist. I have lived a long time, and the righteous Judge has taken good care of me during my whole life. The time has come for my departure, and I long to die and be with Christ. My soul yearns to see Christ, my King, in all his glory." He said many other things which profited us greatly, and so he passed the day joyfully till evening.

When evening came, young Wilbert said to Bede, "Dear master, there is still one sentence that we have not written down."

Bede said: "Quick, write it down."

In a little while, Wilbert said: "There; now it is finished."

Bede said: "Good. You have spoken the truth; it is finished. Hold my head in your hands, for I really enjoy sitting opposite the holy place where I used to pray; I can call upon my Father as I sit there."

And so Bede, as he lay upon the floor of his cell, sang: "Glory be to the Father, and to the Son, and to the Holy Spirit." And when he had named the Holy Spirit, he breathed his last breath.

We believe most firmly that Bede has now entered into the joy of the heaven he longed for, since his labors here on earth were always dedicated to the glory of God.

From the Preface to *Historia Ecclesiastica*, by Saint Bede

My principal authority and aid in the work was the learned and revered Abbot Albinus who was educated in the Church at Canterbury by those venerable and learned men, Archbishop Theodore of Tarsus, of blessed memory, and the Abbot Adrian, and transmitted to me by Nothelm, the godly priest of the Church of London, either in writing or by word of mouth of the same Nothelm, all that he thought worthy of memory that had been done in the province of Kent and adjacent parts by the disciples of the Blessed Pope Gregory I, as he had learned the same either from written records or the traditions of his predecessors. The same Nothelm afterwards went to Rome, where by leave of the present pope, Gregory III, he searched into the archives of the holy Roman Church and found some letters of the blessed Pope Gregory and other popes. Returning home, by the advice of the aforesaid most reverend father Albinus, he brought them to me to be inserted in my history.

Thus the writings of our predecessors from the beginning of this volume to the time when the English nation received the faith of Christ we have collected and from them gathered the material of our history. From that time until the present what was transacted in the Church of Canterbury by the disciples of St. Gregory and their successors and under what kings these things took place has been conveyed to us by Nothelm through the industry of the aforesaid Abbot Albinus. They also partly informed me by what bishops and under what kings the provinces of the East and West Saxons, as also of the East Angles and the Northumbrians received the faith of Christ. In short I was encouraged to undertake this work chiefly by the persuasions of Albinus.

In like manner, Daniel, the most revered bishop of the West Saxons, who is still living, communicated to me in writing some facts regarding the ecclesiastical history of that province and the next adjoining it of the South Saxons, as also the Isle of Wight. And how through the pious ministry of Cedd and Ceadda the province of the Mercians was brought to the faith of Christ, which they had not known before, and how the East Saxons recovered it after having rejected it, and how those fathers lived and died, we learned from the brethren of the monastery which was built by them and is called Lastingham. And what took place in the Church of the province of the Northumbrians from the time they received the faith of Christ until this present, I learned not from any particular writer but from the faithful testimony of innumerable witnesses who might know or remember the same, besides what I had of my own knowledge.

And I humbly entreat the reader that if he find anything in this that we have written not recounted according to the truth, he will not impute the fault to me, who, as the true rule of history requires, have labored sincerely to commit to writing what I could gather from the general report for the instruction of posterity. Moreover, I beseech all men who shall hear or read this history of our nation that for my manifold infirmities of both mind and body they will offer up frequent supplications to the throne of Grace. And I further pray that as reward for the labor wherewith I have recorded for the several countries the events which were most worthy of note and most grateful to the ears of their inhabitants I may have in recompense the benefit of their godly prayers.

From a Commentary on Luke's Gospel, by Saint Bede

"Mary said: My soul proclaims the greatness of the Lord, my spirit rejoices in God my Savior."

The Lord has exalted me by a gift so great, so unheard of, that language is useless to describe it; and the depths of love in my heart can scarcely grasp it. I offer then all the powers of my soul in praise and thanksgiving. As I contemplate his greatness, which knows no limits, I joyfully surrender my whole life, my senses, my judgment, for my spirit rejoices in the eternal Godhead of that Jesus, that Savior, whom I have conceived in this world of time.

"The Almighty has done great things for me, and holy is his name."

Mary looks back to the beginning of her song, where she said: "My soul proclaims the greatness of the Lord." Only that soul for whom the Lord in his love does great things can proclaim his greatness with fitting praise and encourage those who share her desire and purpose, saying: "Join with me in proclaiming the greatness of the Lord; let us extol his name together."

Those who know the Lord, yet refuse to proclaim his greatness and sanctify his name to the limit of their power, "will be called least in the kingdom of heaven." His name is called holy because in the sublimity of his unique power he surpasses every creature and is far removed from all that he has made.

"He has come to the help of his servant Israel for he has remembered his promise of mercy."

In a beautiful phrase Mary calls Israel the servant of the Lord. The Lord came to his aid to save him. Israel is an obedient and humble servant, in the words of Hosea: "Israel was a servant, and I loved him." Those who refuse to be humble cannot be saved. They cannot say with the prophet: "See, God comes to my aid; the Lord is the helper of my soul." But "anyone who makes himself humble like a little child is greater in the kingdom of heaven."

"The promise he made to our fathers, to

Abraham and his children forever."

This does not refer to the physical descendants of Abraham, but to his spiritual children. These are his descendants, sprung not from the flesh only, but who, whether circumcised or not, have followed him in faith. Circumcised as he was, Abraham believed, and this was credited to him as an act of righteousness.

The coming of the Savior was promised to Abraham and to his descendants forever. These are the children of promise, to whom it is said: "If you belong to Christ, then you are descendants of Abraham, heirs in accordance with the promise."

From a Commentary on the First Letter of Peter, by Saint Bede

"You are a chosen race, a royal priesthood." This praise was given long ago by Moses to the ancient people of God, and now the apostle Peter rightly gives it to the Gentiles, since they have come to believe in Christ who, as the cornerstone, has brought the nations together in the salvation that belonged to Israel.

Peter calls them "a chosen race" because of their faith, to distinguish them from those who by refusing to accept the living stone have themselves been rejected. They are "a royal priesthood" because they are united to the body of Christ, the supreme king and true priest. As sovereign he grants them his kingdom, and as high priest he washes away their sins by the offering of his blood. Peter says they are "a royal priesthood"; they must always remember to hope for an everlasting kingdom and to offer to God the sacrifice of a blameless life.

They are also called "a consecrated nation, a people claimed by God as his own," in accordance with the apostle Paul's explanation of the prophet's teaching: "My righteous man lives by faith; but if he draws back, I will take no pleasure in him. But we," he says, "are not the sort of people who draw back and are lost; we are those who remain faithful until we are saved."

In the Acts of the Apostles we read: "The Holy Spirit has made you overseers, to care for the Church of God which he bought with his own blood." Thus, through the blood of our Redeemer, we have become a "people claimed by God as his own," as in ancient times the people of Israel were ransomed from Egypt by the blood of a lamb.

In the next verse, Peter also makes a veiled allusion to the ancient story, and explains that this story is to be spiritually fulfilled by the new people of God, "so that," he says, "they may declare his wonderful deeds." Those who were freed by Moses from slavery in Egypt sang a song of triumph to the Lord after they had crossed the Red Sea, and Pharaoh's army had been overwhelmed; in the same way, now that our sins have been washed away in baptism, we too should express fitting gratitude for the gifts of heaven. The Egyptians who oppressed the people of God, and who can also stand for darkness or trials, are an apt symbol of the sins that once oppressed us but have now been destroyed in baptism.

The deliverance of the children of Israel and their journey to the long-promised land correspond with the mystery of our redemption. We are making our way toward the light of our heavenly home with the grace of Christ leading us and showing us the way. The light of his grace was also symbolized by the cloud and the pillar of fire, which protected the Israelites from darkness throughout their journey, and brought them by a wonderful path to their promised homeland.

CHAPTER 17

SAINT JOHN DAMASCENE

Saint John of Damascus, also known as Saint John
Damascene, is the last of the Fathers and Doctors
of the Church from the East. He is also the first
Doctor from that part of the world for three centuries — since Saint Cyril of Alexandria in the fifth
century.

A lot had happened in those three centuries,
but the most important was the rise of Islam in the
seventh century. Mohammed founded the religion
in Mecca but his flight from there to Medina in 622
is considered to be the beginning of the Islamic
era. Within a century after his death in 632, Islam
spread throughout the Arabian peninsula, across
North Africa, into Spain and as far north and west
as France, throughout the Middle East, and through
Persia to the borders of China.

In the Middle East, the Muslim caliphs ran
into Christian Arabs who could trace their ancestry back to the time of Christ. During the third to
the fifth centuries, Arab Christianity had developed
into the distinctive form of the Syriac Church with
a mature Arab Christian culture, an Arab episco-

pate, Arab monasteries, and an Arabic liturgy. Even after the conquests of the Muslims, there remained active Christian Arab communities, partially because the Muslims administered the conquered territories with great tolerance. In Syria, where Christians had been involved in bitter theological disputes with Byzantine emperors, the coming of Islam was welcomed as an end to tyranny.

This was the situation in Damascus, Syria when John was born there about the year 675. His father, also named John, was one of many Christians who continued to hold important posts as scribes, administrators or architects. The elder John had the position of chief of the revenue department for the caliphate and chief representative of the Christian community — a position that seems to have been hereditary in his family.

A monk called Cosmas, whom the Arabs had captured in Sicily, educated the younger John, teaching him all the sciences, but especially theology. Besides John, Cosmas taught another boy, also called Cosmas, whom the elder John seems to have adopted.

When John grew to manhood, he succeeded his father as chief of the revenue department and representative of the Christian community. In 719, though, when he was in his forties, there was a change in policy among the Muslim rulers. A new caliph decided that he didn't need a representative of the Christian community and he wanted a

Muslim in charge of the revenue department. John lost his position. Along with his friend Cosmas, he entered the Monastery of St. Sabas near Jerusalem and settled down to live the life of a monk. He occupied his time for more than thirty years, when not praying, by writing books and composing hymns.

He turned out to be a prolific author, writing one hundred fifty works on theology, religious education, philosophy, and biographies. His two foremost works were called *Sacred Parallels* and *Fount of Wisdom*. One of three sections of the latter book was called *On the Orthodox Faith*, a summary of the teachings of the Greek Fathers of the Church. St. Thomas Aquinas knew this exposition and, indeed, it has been said that it ranked in importance in the Eastern Church as Thomas's *Summa Theologiae* did in the West. He is also known for his devotion to the Blessed Virgin.

Besides these writings, John became involved in one of the greatest disputes within the Church in the eighth century — Iconoclasm. Icons are representations of Christ, the Blessed Virgin or another saint, painted on a wall or a wooden panel. They were, and are, venerated in Eastern Churches where they take the place of statues, which are venerated in the Western Church.

In the eighth century some eastern Christians came to believe that icons fostered idolatry and that they were prohibited by the biblical ban on

graven images. One of those who became convinced of that was Byzantine Emperor Leo III. In
926 he issued an edict in which he declared that
all images, icons included, were idolatrous and he
ordered them to be destroyed. Thus began what
was called the Iconoclastic Controversy, from a
Greek word meaning "image-breaking."

Naturally, Leo's edict immediately met bitter
opposition, especially from the Eastern Church's
monks, who had long taught the fine art of paint-
ing icons. John wrote three spirited defenses of the
veneration of icons, one in 728 and two more in
730. He made the now-classic distinction between
adoration and worship given only to God and
honor and veneration given to creatures, and he
said that, in cherishing icons, Christians were not
worshiping or venerating the images themselves
but those who were pictured.

His tracts against iconoclasm were widely
circulated and became well known, infuriating the
emperor. Fortunately for John, though, the emperor could not do anything about it because John
was protected inside Muslim territory and he never
crossed the frontier into the Byzantine Empire.

Pope Gregory III condemned iconoclasm in
731 but it remained an issue in the East until long
after John's death. Only after the deaths of three
emperors and the taking of the throne by Empress
Irene in 780 were steps taken to reverse the iconoclastic policies. Finally the Second Council of

Nicaea settled the issue in 787, using some of John's arguments in condemning iconoclasm.

John remained in the monastery for most of his life. At one point, though, the patriarch of Jerusalem, Archbishop John V, called both John and Cosmas out of the monastery, first consecrating Cosmas bishop of Majuma and then ordaining John a priest. John, though, soon returned to the monastery, where he died in 749 at about the age of 74. Pope Leo XIII proclaimed him a Doctor of the Church in 1890.

The Church celebrates his feast on December 4.

From *On the Orthodox Faith*, by Saint John Damascene

Since some find fault with us for worshiping and honoring the image of our Savior and that of Our Lady, and those, too, of the saints and servants of Christ, let them remember that in the beginning God created man after his own image. On what grounds, then, do we show reverence to one another unless it is because we are made after God's image? For as Basil, that much-versed expounder of divine things, says, the honor given to the image passes over to the prototype. Now a prototype is that which is imaged, from which the derivative is obtained.

Why was it that the Mosaic people honored on all hands the tabernacle, which bore an image and type of heavenly things, or rather of the whole creation? God indeed said to Moses, "Look that thou make them after their pattern which was showed thee in the mount." The Cherubim, too, which overshadow the mercy seat, are they not the work of men's hands? What, further, is the celebrated temple at Jerusalem? Is it not hand-made and fashioned by the skill of men?

Moreover, the divine Scriptures blame those who worship graven images, but also those who sacrifice to demons. The Greeks sacrificed and the Jews also sacrificed: but the Greeks to demons and the Jews to God. And the sacrifice of the Greeks was rejected and condemned, but the sacrifice of the just was very acceptable to God. For Noah sacrificed, and God smelled a sweet savor, receiving the fragrance of the right choice and good-will towards him. And so the graven images of the Greeks, since they were images of deities, were rejected and forbidden.

But besides this, who can make an imitation of the invisible, incorporeal, uncircumscribed, formless God? Therefore to give form to the Deity is the height of folly and impiety. And hence it is that in the Old Testament the use of images was not common. But after God in the depths of his bowels of pity became in truth man for our salvation, not as he was seen by Abraham in the semblance of a man, nor as he was seen by the prophets, but in being truly man, and after he lived upon the earth and dwelt among men, worked miracles, suffered, was crucified, rose again and was taken back to heaven, since all these things actually took place and were seen by men, they were written for the remembrance and instruction of us who were not alive at that time in order that though we saw not, we may still, hearing and believing, obtain the blessing of the Lord.

But seeing that not everyone has a knowledge of letters nor time for reading, the Fathers gave their sanction to depicting these events on images as being acts of great heroism, in order that they should form a concise memorial of them. Often, doubtless, when we have not the Lord's passion in mind and see the image of Christ's crucifixion, his saving passion is brought back to remembrance, and we fall down and worship not the material but that which is imaged: just as we do not worship the material of which the Gospels are made, nor the material of the Cross, but that which these typify.

For wherein does the cross, that typifies the Lord, differ from a cross that does not do so? It is just the same also in the case of the Mother of the Lord. For the honor which we give to her is referred to him who was made of her incarnate. And similarly also the brave acts of holy men stir us up to be brave and to emulate and imitate their valor and to glorify God. For as we said, the honor that is given to the best of fellow-servants is a proof of good-will towards our common Lady, and the honor rendered to the image passes over to the prototype.

From *Nativity of the Blessed Virgin Mary*, by Saint John Damascene

Ann was to be the mother of the Virgin Mother of God, and hence nature did not dare to anticipate the flowering of grace. Thus nature remained sterile, until grace produced its fruit. For she who was to be born had to be a first-born daughter, since she would be the mother of the first-born of all creation, "in whom all things are held together."

Joachim and Ann, how blessed a couple! All creation is indebted to you. For at your hands the Creator was offered a gift excelling all other gifts: a chaste mother, who alone was worthy of him.

And so rejoice, Ann, that "you were sterile and have not borne children; break forth into shouts, you who have not given birth." Rejoice, Joachim, because from your daughter "a child is born for us, a son is given us, whose name is Messenger of great counsel and universal salvation, mighty God." For this child is God.

Joachim and Ann, how blessed and spotless a couple! You will be known by the fruit you have borne, as the Lord says: "By their fruits you will know them." The conduct of your life pleased God and was worthy of your daughter. For by the chaste and holy life you led together, you have fashioned a jewel of virginity; she who remained a virgin before, during and after giving birth. She alone for all time would maintain her virginity in mind and soul as well as in body.

Joachim and Ann, how chaste a couple! While safeguarding the chastity prescribed by the law of nature, you achieved with God's help something which transcends nature in giving the world the Virgin Mother of God as your daughter. While leading a devout and holy life in your human nature, you gave birth to a daughter nobler than the angels, whose queen she now is. Girl of utter beauty and delight, daughter of Adam and mother of God, blessed the loins and blessed the womb from which you come! Blessed the arms that carried you, and blessed your parents' lips, which you were allowed to cover with chaste kisses, ever maintaining your virginity. "Rejoice in God, all the earth. Sing, exult and sing hymns." Raise your voice, raise it and be not afraid.

From *On the Orthodox Faith*, by Saint John Damascene

To the saints honor must be paid as friends of Christ, as sons and heirs of God. In the words of John the theologian and evangelist: "But to all who received him, who believed in his name, he gave power to become children of God." So that they are no longer servants, but sons: "and if sons, also heirs, heirs of God and joint heirs with Christ." And the Lord in the holy Gospels says to his apostles: "You are my friends if you do what I command you. No longer do I call you servants, for the servant does not know what his master is doing."...

In the law everyone who touched a dead body was considered impure, but these are not dead. For from the time when he who is himself life and the Author of life was reckoned among the dead, we do not call those dead who have fallen asleep in the hope of the resurrection and in faith in him. For how could a dead body work miracles? How, therefore, are demons driven off by them, diseases dispelled, sick persons made well, the blind restored to sight, lepers purified, temptations and troubles overcome, and how does every good gift from the Father of lights come down through them to those who pray with sure faith? How much labor would you not undergo to find a patron to introduce you to a mortal king and speak to him on your behalf? Are not those, then, worthy of honor who are the patrons of the whole race, and make intercession to God for us?

Yes, truly, we ought to give honor to them by raising temples to God in their name, bringing them fruit-offerings, honoring their memories and taking spiritual delight in them, in order that the joy of those who call on us may be ours, that in our attempts at worship we may not on the contrary cause them offense. For those who worship God will take pleasure in those things whereby God is worshiped, while his shield-bearers will be wroth at those things wherewith God is wroth. In psalms and hymns and spiritual songs, in contrition and in pity for the needy, let us believers honor the saints. Let us raise monuments to them and visible images, and let us ourselves become, through imitation of their virtues, living monuments and images of them.

Let us give honor to her who bore God as being strictly and truly the Mother of God. Let us honor also the prophet John as forerunner and baptist, as apostle and martyr, for among them that are born of women there has not risen a greater than John the Baptist, says the Lord, and he became the first to proclaim the Kingdom. Let us honor the apostles as the Lord's brothers, who saw him face to face and ministered to his passion, for whom God the Father did foreknow he also did predestine to be conformed to the image of his Son, first apostles, second prophets, third pastors and teachers. Let us also honor the martyrs of the Lord chosen out of every class, as soldiers of Christ who have drunk his cup and were then baptized with the baptism of his life-bringing death, to be partakers of his passion and glory: of whom the leader is Stephen, the first deacon of Christ and apostle and first martyr.

Also let us honor our holy Fathers, the God-possessed ascetics, whose struggle was the longer and more toilsome one of the conscience: who wandered about in sheepskins and goatskins, being destitute, afflicted, tormented; they wandered in deserts and in mountains and in dens and caves of the earth, of whom the world was not worthy. Let us honor those who were prophets before grace, the patriarchs and just men who foretold the Lord's coming. Let us carefully review the life of these men, and let us emulate their faith and love and hope and zeal and way of life, and endurance of sufferings and patience even to blood, in order that we may be sharers with them in their crowns of glory.

Saint John Chrysostom: From a Homily on Paul's Letters, January 25; From a Homily on Gospel of John, November 30; From a Homily on Repentance, Tuesday of Twenty-First Week

Saint Ambrose: From the book *On Virginity,* December 13; From *The Explanations of the Psalms,* Saturday of Tenth Week; From *On the Mysteries,* Sunday of the Fifteenth Week

Saint Jerome: From Prologue of Commentary on Isaiah, September 30; From Sermon on Psalm 42, Thursday of Thirteenth Week

Saint Augustine: From a Christmas Sermon, Saturday between Jan. 2 and Epiphany; From Sermon on Christ's Passion, Monday of Holy Week

Saint Cyril of Alexandria: From homily at Council of Ephesus, August 5; From a letter: June 27; From commentary on Gospel of John: Tuesday of Fifth Week of Easter; From a Commentary on the Letter to the Romans: Saturday of Fourth Week of Easter

Saint Peter Chrysologus: From Sermon on Incarnation, July 30; From a Lenten Sermon, Tuesday of Third Week of Lent; From a Sermon, Tuesday of Fourth Week of Easter; From a Sermon, Saturday of Twenty-Ninth Week

Saint Leo the Great: From Christmas Sermon: December 25; From a Sermon, Common of Pastors; From a Sermon, Wednesday of Second Week of Easter

Saint Gregory the Great: From Twenty-Seventh Sunday in Ordinary Time; From Moral Reflections on Job, Friday of Third Week of Lent; From *Dialogues,* February 10; From Homily on the Gospels, Fourth Sunday of Easter

Saint Isidore: From the Book of Maxims, April 4

Saint Bede: From Letter on Death of Bede, May 25; From a Commentary on Luke, December 22

Saint John Damascene: From *Nativity of the Blessed Virgin,* July 26

From *Lives of Saints,* copyright 1954 and 1963 by John J. Crawley & Co.:

Saint Hilary: First excerpt from "On the Trinity." Acknowledgment given to Fathers of the Church, Inc.

Saint Basil: Excerpt from Sermon on Humility. Acknowledgment given to Fathers of the Church, Inc., from *Lives of Saints,* copyright 1954 and 1963 by John J. Crawley & Co.

Saint John Chrysostom: From a homily on the Holy Eucharist. Acknowledgment given to Charles Scribner's Sons for Vol. XIV of *The Nicene and Post-Nicene Fathers, First Series.*

Saint Ambrose: *Morning Hymn* and *Evening Hymn.* Acknowledgment give to F. A. Wright, *Fathers of the Church,* 1928.

Saint Jerome: From Letter to St. Eustochium. Acknowledgment given to F.A. Wright.

Saint Augustine: From *City of God.* Acknowledgment given to translation of John Healey, edition of 1909.

Saint Leo the Great: From the *Tome*: Acknowledgment given to *Letters and Sermons of Leo the Great, Select Library of Nicene and Post-Nicene Fathers, Series II.*

Saint Bede: From Preface to *Historia Ecclesiastica:* Edited by J.A. Giles. Saint Anselm: Two excerpts from *Proslogium*: Translated by S.N. Deane, 1910.

From *The Treasury of Christian Spiritual Classics,* Thomas Nelson Publishers

Saint Augustine: Excerpts from *Confessions.*

From *Saint of the Day* (St. Anthony Messenger Press)

Saint Ephrem: From the Testament of St. Ephrem

Saint Jerome: From Letter to St. Eustochium

From *The Fathers of the Church*
(Our Sunday Visitor)

Saint John Damascene: Two excerpts from *On the Orthodox Faith* taken from 1892 Edinburgh edition
of *The Writings of the Early Church Fathers*.